CRIMINAL TENDENCIES
The Salvatore Luzani Story

Based On A True Story

By Steve Stanley

Copyright © 2011 by Steven A. Stanley

ISBN: 978-0-578-27802-5 (eBook)
ISBN: 978-0-578-27803-2 (Print)

Steve Stanley
1317 Edgewater Drive, #5019
Orlando, FL 32804
305.560.5786
info@criminaltendenciesbook.com

Chapter Listing

About this Book 4

Prologue 5

Chapter One: How To Become a Drug Dealer 7

Chapter Two: The First Run-in With the Mob. 14

Chapter Three: Snowstorm Revenge 20

Chapter Four: Time to die on Welfare Island 24

Chapter Five: I Climb The Ladder 29

Chapter Six: The Promotion 38

Chapter Seven: Time To Go To War 47

Chapter Eight: Betrayed: The Beginning Of The End 54

Chapter Nine: My New Home 60

Chapter Ten: The Great Escape 66

Chapter Eleven: Wanted By the FBI 79

Chapter Twelve: The Long Journey Through Our Criminal Justice System And Beyond! 91

ABOUT THIS BOOK

Buckle-up for the ride of your life! Criminal Tendencies is the true story of Salvatore Luzani, who went from an almost normal high-school student in the suburbs to forming his own paramilitary "crew" and climbing the ladder to become a Top Tier Drug Dealer. He was not shy about taking on any enemy, including the Mob.

He built such a reputation that people knew if they crossed Sal, they would most likely be swimming with the fishes. Readers will be reluctant to put this book down. It is filled with suspense, action, and Sal details everything as it goes down.

Sal always knew he had Criminal Tendencies, but he was losing control of them. People have died, and Sal was tried for 2-counts of First Degree Murder and Acquitted.

You would think that his experience would be enough to straighten him out, but he constantly found himself doing things that were illegal, and he found them exciting and a challenge.

So, get comfortable and enjoy a true crime story about the notorious Salvatore Luzani.

PROLOGUE

At this point in my life, things just weren't going as I had always imagined they would. You know what I'm talking about. We all have this idea about how things will turn out - at least I did, and this just wasn't part of the plan. My life was about to change forever, and there was nothing I could do about it.

I was finally brought to a cell in the older part of the jail. As I am entering this hell hole for the first time, I am quickly greeted by the houseman, who is holding an odd-looking stick. The houseman is the guy in charge of the cell. He's usually somebody who's been in the longest or is considered the toughest dude in the joint. To my great relief, the stick turned out to be the tool he used for turning the channels on the TV, which was located on the other side of the bars. Better that than a whipping stick for new inmates like myself. I no sooner took a deep cleansing breath than I heard: "Hey, this is the guy on the news," the houseman yelled out to the other guys as he took a long hard look at my face.

"Man, you are in some deep shit," he said with a slight laugh. The other inmates, or pre-trial detainees, were all seated around the stainless-steel table in the common area as they looked up at me. They were all watching the news when in I walked. I seemed to be an instant rock star in this godforsaken place, which I figured I could use to my advantage.

I'm not sure if it was that houseman's crooked laugh, or just the realization that I'd be living behind these bars and rooming with a bunch of lunatics for who knows how long, that got me thinking back to when it all began for me - way back to high school and my first hardcore encounters with criminal tendencies.

You see, high school was a transformational experience for me. I entered it as a schmuck and left it as a drug dealer. Please let me explain my story to you.

CHAPTER ONE

How To Become a Drug Dealer

Did it all begin in high school for me, or perhaps much earlier? Well, it's hard to say. What I do know is that high school is where things seemed to change in big ways for me. Not only was I growing up, but the way I saw the world was changing too.

I recall that in my freshman year of high school, I would get punched in the arm all the time as the so-called tough guys would pass me in the halls. Other tough guys would demand money out of me, and there was no doubt I was afraid of them at times. But believe it or not, all that changed after my father bought me a weightlifting set for my fifteenth birthday.

I began to work out like a madman. There were amazing changes in my muscles that really gave me a boost of confidence. After around six months of heavy lifting, my self-esteem had grown leaps and bounds, almost as much as my biceps.

I remember on one particular day; a bad guy came up to me to punch me in my arm once again. I summoned up the guts to sidestep him and give him a super punch in the stomach. I knocked the wind out of him, and he quickly realized that I could have done a lot of damage to him if I had wanted. After that, I gained his respect, and unbelievably, we became good friends. Word quickly got around school not to mess around with me, and that was the beginning. The new me had arrived, and it felt good.

There were other instances in high school where I broke noses, punched teachers, and even rough-handled the assistant principal. I was getting suspended all of the time, and clearly I was becoming a different person.

I was considered an "under achiever," so it seemed that more was always expected of me. I was even given psychological testing for a while, and all the reports came back with the same conclusion: I had Criminal Tendencies.

But even with those criminal tendencies they had discovered, it still felt very good to be in control. I was one of the popular guys, and meeting chicks was easier too. No longer would I be pushed around or extorted. No, now I was the one to be feared. I was the bad guy.

Then one fine day, one of my good friends turned me on to weed. I thought it was the greatest stuff ever invented. You could get as high as you wanted by regulating how much you smoked. Yeah, this was my entry into the world of drugs, and it was great. It wasn't long after that before I realized that I could make good money selling this stuff. I simply needed a good connection for that to become a reality, and then I would turn on the entire high school. Of course, they would pay me well for the privilege.

I was surprised to find out that kids in the honor society smoked weed too. My fellow students were about to see the vast majority of their classmates turn on, thanks to me.

Soon after this, I branched out into LSD, hash, Quaaludes, uppers, and downers. I would take from my mother's prescriptions and sell them to my friends. We had to make the trip to Spanish Harlem in New York City to score pounds of weed. We would take a parking space on 183rd Street, and a guy would ride by on a bicycle and throw the stuff into our car through the window. It was always a little light in weight, but who cares. I would make it up by adding some seeds and stems when I broke it down into smaller units.

After graduation, I lived in my parents' house, while many of my classmates went off to college. I suppose you could say I gave my parents a hard time in those days, there's no doubt about that.

I recall one time when I mixed up a batch of gunpowder from my chemistry set and a spark set the whole bucket of it off. The entire house filled up with a terrible chemical smoke and I had to get my mother out of the house before something even worse occurred. My neighbors thought I was nuts, and maybe I was a little. After all, the experts did say I had criminal tendencies, right?

Then there was that time when I tried to make DMT, a very powerful psychedelic, and a vacuum cleaner exploded and a fire erupted. We thought we were all dying that day for sure. I had placed a padlock on the darkroom door, which was also our little chemistry lab, and a hot plate set off some ether. There was a bright fire flash and no oxygen to breathe. The room filled with the taste of death, and I knew my number was up. I struggled and struggled until I finally managed to get the door opened as we all gasped for breath. The vacuum cleaner exploded because we were using it as an exhaust fan. Pure genius, don't you think?

As it turned out, I did make the stuff, but because I didn't know the correct meaning of "filtrate," I threw the good stuff into the garbage and kept the waste material instead. I still had lots to learn. There's no doubt I kept my parents on their toes back then. I'm sure there were plenty of times they wished I were a normal kid who would go to college someday, get a good job, get married, and have plenty of children. But maybe that was shooting too high. College wasn't for me. I hated that academic shit. The whole 9 to 5 with a wife and kids waiting at home didn't really seem to fit my lifestyle. Hell, I learned more after I got out of high school then I did during the five years I spent there. In fact, I stayed an extra year just to get out of the draft.

You see, the Vietnam War was raging on, and I didn't want to go and get my brains blown out for someone else's profit. I saw a number of my friends come back from Vietnam missing all sorts of body parts, and they weren't quite right in the head either.

That wasn't for me, but the Selective Service System had other ideas. I was Classified as 1A and was going to be drafted. I was ordered to show up at Fort Hamilton for Induction into the Armed Forces. No way! No fucking way! My life was meant for bigger things and I always knew that. No way was I going to go fight in a war I knew nothing about, and risk everything in the process. I asked around and got the name of a psychiatrist who would falsify the psych tests to show I was nuts. For $1,500, he would have me tested by other doctors, and write a report for the draft Board. I was to take this Report with me when I went to Fort Hamilton. Funny that this report also stated that I had "Criminal Tendencies." Maybe they were on to something?

So, all I had to do was act like a sicko, which would be easy for me. I stayed up for three days with hardly any sleep, dressed in all black, and looked as pathetic as I could.

I had refused to board the bus the draft board sent that was supposed to take me to Fort Hamilton. Instead, I drove my car and they did not like that one bit. But screw them. After all, my brain was supposed to be all messed up anyway so my actions fit right in.

When I was finally brought into an interview room, I sat in the very corner of the room trying to look as strange and weird as I could. My goal of course was to make the psychologist a little crazy, and there were a number of ways I thought of to do that. It would all depend on the type of person they seemed to be. Once I figured him out, the rest was easy. I would play the crazy victim. It worked.

The psychologist felt sorry for me. I told him that the draft was like a brick wall in my life, and that I felt like that brick wall was going to crash in on me. When that wall did, I just knew I was going to die. Well, they bought it and I was given a 4-H, which was a Permanent Mental Deferment. I never heard from them again, not once. Many of my friends did the same thing, and they all got out of the draft.

One of my friends had gotten an apartment in New York, and asked me if I wanted to move in. Wow, this would be a chance to get out of my parent's house and move into the big city, cool! My friend supported himself by dealing, and that sounded good to me! Then one day there was a knock at the door. I opened the door, and who is standing there but the guy who was my best friend growing up in Long Island. He had moved into New York with his parents, and we lost touch. "Joey, how the hell are you," I said with a big grin on my face, happy to see my old friend. "What are you doing here? What's Up?" I said.

He was as surprised to see me as I was to see him. Little did I know that he had become a mega-dealer and was supplying my roommate with weed, coke, and Quaaludes? Shit, I loved those Ludes. I used to walk into a club in the city and give out Ludes. Within 20 minutes the whole place was as mellow as could be. You see we had a dentist in New York that would sell us bottles of 500 Ludes for a buck a pill. He was a crazy dentist who liked to whore around, and take advantage of his sedated patients, so he was just the type we were looking for. I just hope he wasn't your dentist. "Sal, I didn't know you lived with Jimmy, that son-of-a-bitch never mentioned your name once. Where the Fuck is he?" my friend said.

I had no idea where he was, but I knew one thing: Jimmy was going to be pissed when he found out, and he was. Now I was in with the main guy, who just happened to be my old best friend. This is going to be sweet. At least that was the plan.

CHAPTER TWO

The first run-in with the mob.

We've all seen the movies. You know the ones, "The Godfather," "Goodfellas," "The Sopranos." We've watched those movies and all wondered if things were really as brutal out there as these movies portray. Well, I'm here to tell you that they are. In fact, I'll take that a step further: movie bad guys are pussies compared to the real life bad guys. You see the real-life bad guys aren't actors and don't have a script in front of them. Everything they do is out of impulse and reaction and sometimes they just flat out get it wrong. But unlike the movies, when real bad guys get it wrong, they die for real.

In June 1973, I had rented a small store on Northern Boulevard in Flushing, New York. This would be a front for my drug dealing activities in this area. Downstairs was a very old, creepy basement. We turned it into a target practice room so that we could sharpen our gun skills. Gun skills were a very important part of my new business endeavors. Without gun skills you would most likely become a victim rather than a victor. I worked very hard on my skills and became pretty good at shooting from the hip.

I set up a working chemical lab in the back room. There was a chemist who was going to make all the LSD I wanted. All the chemicals were available from chemical companies, but you had to be a company to make the purchase. I came up with the idea that I would use the chemical name for meth, Dextro Desoxyphedrine-Hydrochloride, and try to buy it from a chemical company. This would be much easier than attempting to manufacture LSD, and more profitable. I used stolen purchase orders that were obtained from a break-in on a business, we just changed the name and address.

At first I bought some run-of-the-mill chemicals from several different companies just to get things going. Then later it was time to get the real stuff. I got a call from Aldrich Chemical Company in Wisconsin. They wanted to know why I needed this item. I explained that I was in the process of filing a patent for a new chemical process for Sepia Toning Photographs. I said I could not disclose the process, but that this chemical was a vital component of the formula. Those morons at Aldrich Chemical bought my story, and soon I was receiving cartons with glass bottles of 100 percent pure meth! It could be cut several times and still be killer stuff. All you had to do was break the seal, open the jar, and take a whiff. The crystals floating up would give you a buzz, this was incredible shit.

Moving this stuff was the next order of business. I wasn't used to dealing with meth freaks. They were a whole different kind of people. They were clearly addicted to the stuff and you never really know what was going to happen with them.

One of my people knew some guys that were vouched for, that could make a $50,000 sample purchase. If they liked it, there would be larger buys. I approved the deal and set a place for it to go down. A family member ran a kitchen cabinet factory called Peerless-Mayer, Inc., in Hunts Point, which was located in the Bronx. This was not a nice place to be sure. Garbage littered the streets. Junk yards were across the street. Gangs of wild dogs were roving all over the place. They called this place Fort Apache, and for good reason. We could drive into the building and do our business and then leave. It sounded like a simple deal.

So, I met with my guys at the store. We knew we would be armed for the deal. It was a big deal, and we were wary of the buyer. Only one guy vouched for them. Everybody carried their weapons of choice. I had my 9mm, a bullet proof vest, and a .38 caliber strapped to my ankle. The deal was to go down at 10 p.m. on Tuesday night. This meant that we would get there at 9 p.m. to check it out and secure the area.

I had a key to the building, and so did my friend who set it up. The deal was to meet at the Hunts Point Diner at 9:30 p.m., so I could check them out. My friend would call me at 10 p.m. at the factory for the OK to come on over. We had it all figured out and what could possibly go wrong, right?

We arrived on the scene in three vehicles. An initial pass of the building revealed some vehicles that did not belong there. We parked down the block at a junk yard and observed with binoculars. Five guys arrived and entered the building. This looks like a set-up, an inside job in the making.

This stinks, I thought. Not much time to think, I figured. We had to make a move quickly because they could be ripping off our guy. We decided to enter the building from two points. The paint spray booth ductwork was installed with quick disconnects for service. I would enter through there with Carlos and Larry. Mario, Jimmy, and Vinny would go in through a restroom, way in the back of the factory. There were hundreds and hundreds of boxes full of kitchen cabinets piled up all around. It would be easy to sneak about unobserved, and very easy to knock something over and make noise. We all had to be very careful.

In the shop foreman's office, we could see a bunch of guys sitting around a table snorting some blow. I heard one of them say this would be easy money. I gave my guys the signal, and it was time to rock and roll! I pulled my 9mm out and kicked open the door, followed by my crew, with Mario securing the area outside the office. "Everybody freeze! Get down on the floor and just maybe we won't put a slug in your fucking heads," I yelled in the most menacing voice I could muster.

We had them face down on the floor as we searched them for guns and ID. They sure looked like a bunch of Italians.

"Are you fucking crazy?" one of them yelled. "Do you know who we are?"

"No!" I yelled back. "But if you don't keep your mouth shut, you won't be anybody anymore, Capeche?"

The phone rang. It was my friend who set this up.

"Sal, I am at the Hunts Point Diner. The guys must still be at the factory securing it for themselves."

I said to myself: "Are you shitting me?"

"Why didn't you tell me you asshole? Who are these guys anyway?" I said to my friend.

"They are connected with Galantino's family," he replied.

"You better get your ass over here quick and identify them, or I will dust them all!"

I was getting a sick feeling in my gut. I didn't want a war with the mob. If this were a mistake, we would have some time getting out of this mess. My friend finally arrived.

"Sal, these are my guys, what the fuck are you doing?" my friend yelled.

"How the hell was I supposed to know they would be here early, this was not the plan, was it?" I said, feeling sicker with every word.

"No, but they insisted. Sorry Sal, Sorry guys," my friend said.

I had to do something.

"OK, everybody shut the fuck up," I said. "This is what we are going to do, we are going to lower our Roscos, and nobody gets killed."

We lowered our weapons, but Mario kept a trained eye on what was going down. The guns were returned along with their wallets. I apologized profusely and asked them to join us for a drink, some blow and a joint. After a little while, we were all laughing about the incident.

"Sal, you guys are something else. You caught us with our pants down, and we know you could have iced all of us," said Pasquale, their lead man. "You have earned our respect here today for the way you guys handled this situation, it could have been ugly"

All the while my friends were also cooling them down. These wise guys hadn't been up against a criminal organization like ours before, and I think it really shocked them. You see, all that practice in that basement really paid off for us, along with the fact that we were built with military discipline, using guys from Vietnam that were trained in all of the killing arts, and very proficient. This is the new criminal organization. It's not just the mob anymore. We all made it home alive that night, so it was a very good day.

CHAPTER THREE

Snowstorm Revenge

When you live a life of crime you plan on being the one doing the crime, not the one who has the crime done to them. It's almost insulting when that happens. I mean, we're the bad guys, right? We go after everybody else, and isn't there supposed to be an unwritten Code of Ethics between us? Honor amongst thieves, and all that shit? Aren't we supposed to stick it to the victims but treat each other fairly with a certain level of respect? Well, maybe that's the way it happens in the movies, but that's not how it works out there on the streets. In fact, sometimes we go out of our way to screw our fellow criminals.

I remember it was when Long Island was hit by a massive snowstorm. A lot on the ground with more on the way. I had just gotten out of bed and was having my morning coffee and a joint when the phone rings. It was Joey.

"Sal, is this a joke?" he said. "Are you out of your fucking mind? Do you think I am stupid?"

I am in shock because I don't know why Joey is so pissed off.

"Why did you give me counterfeit money? I thought I could trust you," he added.

"Hey, slow down man. I wouldn't knowingly give you bogus bills," I said.

"Sal, you have 24-hours to make me whole," he said, with a more serious tone.

Sure, this guy may have been my friend, but he loved money way more then he loved me. I had heard stories about what happens to guys who cross him, and they weren't very nice stories either, if you know what I mean.

"OK. OK. I know exactly who gave me that stuff. I will make good for the $36K, relax!" I said.

I had just done a deal with some guys from Great Neck, not too far from where I was based. It's great that it is still snowing. I was getting myself all worked up over this - imagine those son-of-a-bitches not giving a shit if I ended up getting dusted. Time for a new mission. If I call these Great Neck guys they can hide the weed I sold them and get rid of the real money. They placed my life in jeopardy, they don't deserve a break.

I called a few of my guys and explained to them what just happened. They were excited about this mission in the snow. I put some cinder blocks in my trunk, put on snow chains, and drove by their house to scope it out.

One thing to keep in mind is to always know the layout of the place you are going to hit. Remember that for when you become a drug dealer! A professional scopes out every place he goes. I make mental notes of every window, points of entry and all exits.

This will be a home invasion type of mission. We will take control of the place and take everything of value. Those guys will take their punishment, or they will die! It's that simple.

We waited until dark. These guys are not big timers, but if they resist, they will be dusted. We rolled out at about 10 p.m. All of us were smashed and ready for action. I parked down the block after I dropped two guys around the back street. We were all dressed in white and blended in beautifully. I would go up to the front door, crouch down, and tell them some bullshit story to get them to open the door. Meanwhile, my guys are coming in through the kitchen door.

I knock on the front door.

"It's your neighbor, I need help, I think my Dad had a heart attack," I yelled. The door opens and I nail him in the face while smashing him up against the nearest wall.

"Tell everybody to cool it, and nobody dies tonight. Your choice." They knew why we were there.

Meanwhile, Larry had two guys on the floor in the bedroom. Vinny was punching one of these wise guys on the ground. We finally got everybody in one room, on the floor. Larry takes the leader and cracks him on the head with his pistol. Blood goes flying everywhere as the guy cringes on the floor. I hate trying to get rid of blood stains, they never seem to come all the way out. I should wear coveralls for these types of missions.

He says he will make it right, that it was not his idea. His friend had the counterfeit bills to get rid of.

"How dare you make a fool out of me! I should ice you right now," I said. He begged for his life. We ransacked the place and found about $45,000 in good bills, and most of the weed, plus a bonus. He also had 10,000 Quaaludes. We left the guys on the ground with their hands tied behind them. Let them figure out how to escape. Fuck them.

I leaned over and whispered in the leader's ear.

"If I even hear that you are looking for us, you, and your family are dead."

By now we had the reputation for turning threats into reality. Nobody died tonight. We got the money. It was a good night, and another victory for the good guys - or should I say bad guys - so I thought.

CHAPTER FOUR

Time to die on Welfare Island

Sometimes you can do everything right and still the plan goes to hell in a handbag. Even bad guys have bad days, and I seemed to have a lot of them lately. The only difference is when we have bad days, people die.

It was a very cold winter night in 1975. Snow was on the ground with more to come. I don't know why, but I always liked to see deals go down in the snow. This would be one to remember, or forget, depending on your perspective.

Ever hear of Welfare Island? It is a spooky island between Queens and Manhattan. The only way on or off is a bridge from Long Island City. When you arrive on the island, it is like going back in time. This was a place with hospitals and a mortuary, and I suppose sometimes the two go together. It was all abandoned as if there was a cataclysmic event and everyone died or something. There were even wooden wheelchairs and patient gurneys sitting around. Sometimes we would bring broads up there and get high and have wild sex in the hospital lounge, but that's another story.

In the mortuary were complete cases of autopsied individuals preserved in formaldehyde left in large porcelain containers. There was even a storage area with handwritten ledger style cause-of-death journals. I could read where people died from syphilis. This was old stuff. The place was creepy as hell but was a great place to take acid, which I did on more than one occasion. I once used a machete to dissect a human brain. It looked like cauliflower. Only crazies and criminals come to this place, so I suppose we were in the right place. Tonight, we are here to do a Quaalude deal.

We know every inch of this place, especially the hospital with its elaborate circular staircase leading up to the upper floors. The deal was set. First we meet up with some wise guys from Staten Island who would have 20,000 ludes for 40 cents each. I could sell them for $5.00 each all day long. Then we would meet up with some guys from a Puerto Rican Gang from the Bronx. Gotta watch those gangs, they have no codes.

The first part of the deal took place in the operating room on the second floor on the north side of the building. It went down smooth. The ludes weighed out OK. You can't count pills one at a time, you have to weigh them.

That night, we rolled with seven guys in our crew. We weren't taking any chances. Guys would be positioned around the scene with two-way radios. I told everyone to wear a vest. The buyers were supposed to arrive around 11 p.m.. We were hanging around, getting buzzed, just waiting, under candlelight.

The two-way radio starts making sounds. Tiny, one of my guys, was in trouble.

"Sal, I'm down. Been stabbed. They're on the way up!" he said as his agonized voice trailed off.

It turned out he didn't wear his vest. This means that we are under attack. All of my men heard this call for help. We had candles we were using for light, so we blew them out. The light from the skylights was enough for this operation. It was a good thing there was a full moon tonight.

This was a textbook attack. They took out our sentry in silence. Now they were coming for us, but we weren't born yesterday. This was a war zone. The standard plan was to position ourselves so that we could ambush the attackers.

We waited in silence for them to close in on our position. I was behind a nurses station with two of my guys, Larry, and Carlos. Each of us were ready to open fire as there was no need to be shy. You could set off a bomb and nobody would hear it. Cops never came here, and you were on your own in this place.

We could make out three figures heading in, very low to the ground. We knew it was none of our men. I opened fire, and the popping sound of my gun echoed throughout the room. Carlos had a sawed-off shotgun, and he blasted the mother fuckers. They were hit so hard that it lifted one of them off his feet. Mario opened fire with his .9mm. At the same time, we heard gunfire downstairs. It sounded like a fire fight in Vietnam. I suppose I ended up in a war after all, but this war was of my own making. I didn't know what the hell was happening. All I knew was that now the element of time comes into play. We will need to sanitize this place - get rid of bodies and take the wounded to our doctors who handle this type of stuff. I hear the sounds of feet coming up the stairs. It looked like Jimmy was holding a gun on some creep.

"Sal, everything is secure downstairs. I have a present for you. Here is the Rat," Jimmy said.

It turned out it was one of our friends, or so we thought he was one of friends. I told Jimmy to step aside. I level my Rosco point blank at the Rat's forehead and provided his skull with ventilation. He drops like a sack of shit. Then, Jimmy tells me that Tiny is dead.

We lost one of our own that night. We all know what happened there, what we needed to do - fast. This isn't the first time we operated on Welfare Island, and it wouldn't be the last.

Larry got the body bags out of the morgue. They were old but would work just fine. We weighed them down and brought them to the water's edge on the wooden gurneys. Tiny had to get dumped in the water with the other five bodies. I felt bad for him. Nobody would ever know what happened to him, and that was a sad thing. But we all knew how things worked if we died.

It was "Time to swim with the fishes," as they say. It wasn't a very good night.

CHAPTER FIVE

I Climb The Ladder

Of course, the life of a drug dealer entrepreneur is filled with fast cars, fast women, and lots of money, if you play your cards right. Don't get me wrong, it's also filled with lots of death, despair, and stress, but you know the old saying, "If you can't stand the heat, get out of the kitchen." There are those upsides to living a life of crime for sure, but there is also a price to be paid. Perks that just seem to follow lots of money and drugs always come with a price tag at the end of the day.

So here I am in Joey's Penthouse on the Upper East Side celebrating my 22nd birthday. That's right, only 22, and my life so far made most of Al Pacino's movies look like children's flicks. He would shit in his drawers if he lived one day in my life.

Joey made sure there would be all kinds of beautiful women there, and he knew how much I liked black chicks. I was gonna have a good time tonight. I would have all the weed I could smoke, Ludes, and all the coke I could snort. This must be heaven. I thought to myself, this is the way I want to live. That night I promised myself that I would go big time and nobody was going to get in my way. I didn't care how long it took, or who got stepped on, I would make it to the top or die trying. Sounds kind of like and old James Cagney movie doesn't it?

"Hey Sal, I'd like you to meet Lisa," Joey said with a huge grin on his face.

Lisa, a fine black chick, was my birthday present.

"Hi Lisa. You look incredible tonight," I said.

I was speechless. It was the only line I could come up with on the spot. She was so beautiful, with smooth features and a nice ass. I was really going to have fun. I brought her out on the terrace, and we smoked a joint and took a Lude. It wasn't long before we were in a guest bedroom. I'll never forget that night. We were inseparable after that evening. I could really fall for this chick, and I knew it. She knew how to take care of a man, and how to make him feel like a king.

The next day, Joey wanted to have a meeting with me. He was going to make a buy from some guys he didn't trust and wanted me to be there packing heat. He handed me a .38 caliber snub nose pistol, a nice looking Rosco. Joey didn't know the extent of my experience with guns and that I was a deadly waste-high shooter, and maybe that was a good thing.

These wise guys controlled the coke around this area, and they had the best. You could buy coke from other dealers, but it wouldn't be as pure. It has to be pure so you can cut it down. Joey trusted me. He knew I would take a bullet for him, or so he thought, and that was OK, too. He would have other guys with him, but he trusted me above all. He knew I had the balls needed to take care of any situation.

"If you do this for me, I will take care of you," he said with a grin.

"When you need me, you can count on me. If I have to ice somebody, consider it done," I replied.

I thought to myself, what did I just say. Am I nuts? I didn't know how he would take care of me, but I figured what the hell, he will owe me one at the very least. Another thing this business is all about is taking chances - all sorts of chances, and not all of them with guns.

Sure enough, we go to do the deal and they try to give us a light count. This happens too often. Either they will try to give you a light count or give you some very cut stuff. We once got coke cut with baking soda. We had muffins coming out of our noses. This is why we use our own scales.

We met in a warehouse in Long Island City on Van Dam Street. There were three of them and three of us. I learned growing up to always watch the hands. I saw Gino moving his hand toward the small of his back.

"Freeze motherfucker," I said.

I pulled my piece out and pointed it at his head.

"You go for that gun and I will put a slug in your skull," I said with a maniacal look on my face.

He stopped moving his hand. I checked his back and sure enough he had a .380 automatic tucked away in his belt. Joey and Larry pulled out their pieces. Now things are gonna be different. It was obvious to me they were going to rip us off.

"Joey, take your shit, leave them their money and we are going to leave. Nobody has to die here today," I said.

I was thinking it wasn't gonna be me that was going to die for sure.

The other guys made up some excuse why it was light, and we backed out of the place with guns in hand. I had a feeling we would meet up with them again someday. Joey was very impressed with the way I took over the situation. He wanted me to be his capo. I would be in on every major deal with my crew for protection. Sometimes we were referred to as "The Luzani Crew." If you wanted tight security, you wanted us. We were like the bad guy A-Team or something.

I had built up my own crew over the years. I had several friends that would do anything: the crazier the better. They had no fear, and that was perfect. Some of them had been in Vietnam and had some special talents, like Larry, who they called "Loco Larry." From this point on, things would be different.

I never saw so much cash at one time as the night I came over to the penthouse and saw a king-size bed totally covered with cash. There was well over one million dollars on the bed. Holy Shit! The thought ran through my mind that I could just ice everybody and take the cash, but that was a little too far out at this point, even for me. Maybe in the future.

Larry had put a deal together and a bunch of buyers were in town. A couple of truckloads of weed from Florida were on their way to the Upstate New York workhouse, and we needed to beef up security. There would be about 5,000 pounds of high-grade Colombian marijuana in 40-pound bales. This should be fun. I was able to buy weed at the wholesale cost in any quantity. My cost was as good as the cost for the big guys with the big bucks. I had my own customers to supply as a result of dealing for years and years, and that was a good thing. I knew everybody, so life was good. "Sal, I want you to go upstate with your crew, and secure the place tight. Nobody gets in or out unless you know about it. Make sure everybody is packing heat, and have the two-way radios," Joey said.

There is always the chance of a rip-off somewhere along the lines. This is why Joey had about eight workhouses. He had places in Upstate New York, Long Island, Florida, and Philadelphia. If he had a workhouse set up, he was dealing drugs through it, and making huge amounts of cash. We did a lot of traveling in those days and saw a lot of crazy shit. This was some place. The freaking driveway went on forever. It was on 16 acres. I thought to myself how this place was too big to secure. It was crazy. I would need an army for this job. All we could do is patrol a tight perimeter around the house and garage. We went early so we could figure out where to place my men. I would have six guys on the grounds. Four would be static, and two would be on the move, checking the grounds around the house. We would keep in touch over the two-ways. Larry brought a couple of sets of night vision gear.

The police were not the problem as they were paid off. It was the other assorted nuts you had to worry about. The wise guys that wanted to make a name for themselves.

You never knew who might have said something to some broad when they were high. Some people don't know the meaning of "Keep your mouth shut." More secrets have been spilled because of booze than you could imagine. And remember, "Hell Hath No Fury Like A Women Scorned." You know what that means? It means keep your business to yourself and don't tell your old lady or you may live to regret it. Or should I say, you will die to regret it.

> The Weed Trucks arrived at about 8 p.m. Larry spotted them entering the grounds and called me on the two-way.

> "Sal, open the Gates, they're here," he told me.

> "Okay, you guys close in behind them, leave Carlos at the Gazebo and have him set-up for the night. And make sure you guys have vests on," I said.

The trucks came in and were unloaded into the basement without a hitch. Now each Bale had to be weighed, numbered, and logged. This would take 3-4 hours. We could now schedule the arrival of the buyers.

There were to be four cars with a buyer and his second. They were instructed not to be strapped, but they would be patted down before they could enter the premises.

It's midnight, and they are starting to arrive, four cars are here. Carlos gets on the two-way and says, "There is another car heading in, I thought there were four fucking cars, what gives."

"There are at least four guys in the car," he added.

"I want them stopped before they get to the Gate," I said.

"Jimmy, pull a vehicle out to block the road, and fast, Pete and Vinny flank their car. Hold them and wait for me," I ordered.

This was not good, and I was starting to get that bad feeling in my gut again. It wasn't going to be a fun evening on this cold winter night in the Catskills, and I already knew it. We knew right away what is going on.

"POP, POP, POP," I hear as I head for the intercept. Larry gets on the two-way. "Carlos is hit, I hope he had his fucking vest on, small arms fire, we have them pinned down behind some trees," he said in an adrenalin-charged voice.

"I am on the way with Mario, let's not shoot each other, all lights out, night vision only," I barked.

It's as cold as a witch's tit and I had no gloves. The vests keep in some warmth though. There will be no warnings given tonight. We came up very quickly on these assholes. I had my piece pointed and ready, I emptied my clip into these amateurs. Good thing I brought my 9mm instead of the .38. I dusted two of them, my other guys dusted the rest. Now there were four dead guys to identify and dispose of, and this means a bonus.

"Joey, everything is under control here. Nobody leaves until I check everyone out. We have four stiffs to get rid of, and one of them is Gino," I said.

"Sal, you know he is connected with the Gambino Family; this isn't good, we don't want to go to war with Gambino", he replied back, clearly a little shaken.

"They opened fire first, and were here to fucking rob us, Carlos got hit" I said.

"Carlos had his vest on; he is OK, but his ribs are all bruised," I added.

Now we have to do a quick clean up, as we have done before. Larry loves body bags. We stuff them into Body Bags and throw them into a van to be buried. You want to know where we buried them? Forget about it! All the buyers were brought into the garage and I addressed the group.

"As you heard, there was an attempted rip-off tonight. Nobody is leaving here until I say so; somebody either set this up or was followed. I will find out which it is, and scores will be settled. Not a promise, a guarantee," I said in a pissed off voice.

Now all of the weed must be re-loaded onto the trucks and brought to another workhouse. And fast. Everybody must help, but nobody will know where the shit is going. No communications are allowed, these are the rules. Joey will arrange a sit-down with a representative from the Gambinos. It's the only way to keep things from getting out of hand, and by getting out of hand I mean we could all end up swimming with those fishes if things aren't handled right. It will be great when this night is over, I thought.

CHAPTER SIX

The Promotion

And then just when everything seems to be falling into place, you have the rug pulled right out from under you. It wasn't like I went into this line of work planning on climbing the proverbial drug kingpin ladder; but there is a structure, a sort of company structure that is observed and even sometimes coveted. But what it really boils down to is respect. Being given the right amount of respect in this business is very important. Respect is the difference between being a victim and being a leader. People die over respect all the time.

So I get a phone call from Joey's partner, Carmine.

"When we meet at the Queens Office, Joey is going to announce his new under boss, be cool"

"Okay, I will be there with bells on."

This means that at the next weed distribution, somebody is getting bumped up the ladder.

I wondered why Carmine said to "be cool." What the hell did that crack mean? Everybody knows it is going to be me! After all, Joey and I grew up together, went to high school together, robbed houses together. Hell, we used to bring chicks back to his parent's house and get laid all of the time. Joey and I were tight, right? I saved Joey's ass many times; I stuck my neck out for that guy! It damn well better be me!

It's a beautiful Spring Day. Great day to get the key to the city, I thought. This will be sweet. We all met at a rented house in Corona, just off the Long Island Expressway. There were about six buyers there with their soldiers.

After business is done, Joey brings out a silver serving tray covered with a couple ounces of coke for the boys, and some booze. It seemed it was going to be a great day.

"Everybody, gather around, I have big news tonight," Joey said.

Big Lou is going to step up and stand beside me. This means he is "The Man, not me." Big Lou was cool, but it should have been me! Big Lou was about 285 pounds, standing 6 feet 6 inches tall and was solid muscle. His neck was bigger than my thigh. Steroids will make your momma big too. Yeah, he was bigger than me, but you wanna see how fast he drops with a bullet in his scull?

The other guys all looked at each other. They knew it should have been me. Now I remember when Joey once said I was too ambitious. He must have been afraid I might someday make a move against him. I am very pissed at this point and everybody there knew it! Joey just made a huge mistake; he just didn't know it yet.

I will get even with him. This is bullshit! I couldn't let everybody see how angry I was. I could have just iced him right then and there, but that might not work out the best. I needed to give this whole thing some thought. Remember – "Revenge is best served cold."

It didn't take long before I came up with a plan. The next time we offload a weed shipment from Columbia to our Miami workhouse, we will stage a rip-off. Me and my girl will set it up on the inside and make like we are one of the victims. This has to be done with care, or we all will be swimming with the fishes.

I discussed this with my crew. They were as pissed off as I was and were always eager to have some fun. Days go by, my crew starts getting all the gear together and staging some practice runs. Everybody is eager to do this because it could be a good payday.

So I get the call telling me that there will be work on Saturday. This means that there is a mother ship on its way to Miami. Planes will be sent out to get the latitude and longitude, and high speed Donzi's will go out and offload the bails of weed.

It will be brought to shore in the Keys and transported in Conversion Vans to the Coral Gables workhouse. Most of my crew will come down to Florida for this job. They will be given two-way radios and will hide outside of the house. If there were any sentries posted around the house, they would all be neutralized. When Lisa goes to the bathroom, she will unlock the door to the pool and light a joint by the window. This would be a signal to wait a couple of minutes and come in like gang busters. Nobody will get hurt if this is done right. This is going to be an armed robbery and it should be fun. At least that was the plan.

The weed had arrived in six vans and was brought into all of the bedrooms and stacked up to the ceiling. The place stunk like burlap. There were a couple of paper shopping bags in the kitchen cabinets with a lot of cash - several hundred thousand bucks in total.

The weed quality was not the best, but free was a good price. I had rented a safe house in Margate. This is where we would meet and make the splits. My guys would take the cash, and as much weed as they could get in the rented van.

At the right moment, I gave Lisa the nod. She headed into the master bedroom's bathroom and gave the signal. There was no turning back now. I remember how I felt this incredible adrenalin rush.

We were all sitting around in the living room watching TV, making jokes, smoking weed. I made sure my back was to the hallway that they would enter through.

"Freeze mother fuckers! Everybody on the floor! You make a move, you die!" my guys yelled. They burst into the room with guns drawn. They looked good in ski masks and scared the shit out of me too. I see Ken's face turn from a smile to sheer terror. I thought, wow, this is really happening, I am ripping off my boss. It sure felt good, and that fuck had it coming.

I guess Lou picked a bad night to buy some weed. One of my guys escorts Lisa into the room and orders her to the ground. She looks pretty shaken, but I knew I would make it up to her. Everybody had their hands cuffed with those plastic tie wraps. Now my guys have to find out where the cash is, and I can't tell them. You Dig? Larry grabs one of the guys by the hair, points the gun between his eyes, and says,

"Where is the fucking cash? You can all die here tonight, or you can give up the cash, and we will be on our way." Larry said.

But Joey wasn't going down without a fight.

"Do you know who I am, you assholes?" Joey blurts out.

Larry hits him with his 9mm on the back of his head.

"Yeah, you're the guy who just got hit in the back of the head. Want more Mr. Big Stuff?" My guy sounded funny in his disguised voice. I figured I should show some resistance.

So I yelled. "Leave him alone. Payback is a bitch"

Carlos grabs me by the shoulder and stands me up.

"You're coming with me." He took me into the kitchen, gave me a fake punch in the stomach, and let me drop to the floor. I moved my eyes in the direction of the cabinets with the cash. I should have won an Emmy for this performance.

I am brought out into the garage, which was also full of weed. Now I need some marks on me to make this look really good.

Carlos whispers into my ear.

"Sorry Sal," and then backhands me in the face. He busted my lip, but the blood looked good. He opens the garage door for Jimmy and Pete to load up the bails of weed, and brings me back into the living room, throws me down on the floor with blood all over my face by now.

"You okay, Sal? Whoever set this up will die," Joey said with total resolve in his angry voice.

Carlos makes like he is searching the kitchen and comes across the cash and a surprise. It was a one-pound bag of cocaine! All we had to do was get through this mission and it was going to be a really good night.

Vinny steps over me as I lay on the floor stomach down. He makes sure nobody is looking, as they were all preoccupied with Mario threatening them with death if they make a move. As they leave, he cuts my cuffs so I can make like I pulled off a miraculous escape to run into my bedroom to get my Rosco and take control of the situation. Now I am thinking, what if one of them wants to see my plastic cuffs to see how I broke them. I need to get rid of them no matter what.

If I am put on the spot, I may have to dust everybody, and that could get messy. You know how I hate to clean up blood. I ran like a bat out of hell and got my gun. Then I cut Lisa free and told her to cut everyone's cuffs. I yelled to Joey that I was going outside to secure the grounds, which is standard for this type of situation.

Joey had provided his own security today, but they are nowhere to be found. I wonder what could have happened to them. Do you have any ideas? I guess they didn't do too well. Everybody got out of there fast. No police will be called. The house had to be emptied; it will never be used again. Joey was pissed. Plenty of people have disappeared for pulling this type of shit!

Joey headed back to the Mutiny Hotel in Coconut Grove to meet up with his partner, Carmine. Wait till Carmine hears about this night. I met up with the boys at the Margate safe house. We each took our share and headed north to Hartford, Conn. I had some people there that would take the weed. I wanted to avoid dumping it in the city.

My share was about $360,000, and 400 pounds of weed and four ounces of snow. All in all, a good days work. Next, me and Lisa headed for our crib in the Big Apple. After the rip-off, everybody was paranoid, and there was not too much action happening.

We used to hang out at the jazz clubs downtown, like Boomers and Slugs. One day, outside of a club, in the not too distant future, I bump into Freddy Big Lip, one of Joey's Soldiers. He had one lip bigger than the other, looked like a freaking goon.

"Joey wants to see you, now. You're coming with me Sal."

Imagine that, this schmuck thinks he is going to put the grabs on me.

"Sorry, but I got plans and going with your ugly ass isn't one of them," I said.

I kept walking. Then he made a big mistake. He grabbed me by the shoulder, and I did a Judo move and then a right cross direct on his chin, followed up with a front kick to his knee. He drops to his knees in pain as I knee him in the face.

"Tell Joey I will give him a call," I said, smiling.

Now Freddy can add a broken nose to his big lip. Too bad for him. They should call him: "Freddy Big Lip With Broken Nose." I kept walking as I straightened out my clothes.

Later I gave Joey a call and told him his guy was out of line, and he knows how I react when someone tries to put the grabs on me, but that I am always available to meet with him if I know where and when. Now I am told that everyone there will be required to take a polygraph given by an ex-Miami detective that was on the payroll.

This was bad news. There was no way me or Lisa will pass the polygraph. If we fail the test, we are as good as dead. Other people have been dusted before for the same reason. I needed a plan as this was very bad. In fact, it was the absolute worst-case scenario for me. Me and my girl could be killed over this shit, and I wasn't going to let that happen.

CHAPTER SEVEN

Time To Go To War

So the plan worked like a charm, but things were getting a bit sticky. It's like telling a lie; once you tell one you usually need to tell ten more just to keep the one alive. Well that's what I was up against. The ripple effect of my actions was following me around like a pit bull. It looked like I was going to be very busy in the next few days. It looked like more people were going to die, and I just wanted to make sure that I wasn't one of them.

When I went down to Florida, everybody was planning on taking the polygraph.

"Be available!" Joey had said 10 minutes ago.

This is it, time for survival mode to kick in and I knew it. The only way I can stop this in its tracks is to ice one of the bosses. They will all shit in their drawers; they won't know who is next. They will back off. I had been thinking about it and came up with a plan.

I needed a disguise and silencers for sure. I couldn't buy a silencer and nobody can know anything. I will have to learn how to make a silencer, which sounded like a fun job. My Resume could say something like "Makes great silencers." It sounds crazy, but that was the kind of life I was living. Like I said before, Al Pacino movies had nothing on me. This was for real, but I couldn't just dust Joey. I grew up with him. I just couldn't do it. Carmine is the one who will be dusted since I never liked him anyway.

I decided to set up another safe house in Fort Lauderdale and Florida has gun stuff everywhere. I picked up a copy of "Soldier of Fortune" magazine and saw an ad for Paladin Press. They had books on everything, including how to make a silencer. I need to set up a mini-machine shop in the safe house, where I would learn, experiment, and implement.

I found a place in downtown New York where I could get a Unimat Lathe. This thing is a miniature metal working machine that can do everything I need to do. Good thing I was always mechanically inclined. I also found the address of a theatrical supply house in New York that could make me a beard and mustache.

Here was the plan: First, I flew to Philadelphia and bought some books on making silencers. Then, I flew to New York City to buy the Unimat Lathe and get fitted for a quality beard and mustache. Then, I bought some guns that were the easiest to equip. We would also use bulletproof vests in case we had to shoot our way out of this mess. I had to get some .22 caliber pistols of the kind the CIA has used in the past.

After I figured out how to make a silencer, my plan was to hit Carmine at his home in Coral Springs, Florida. I knew the layout well, and he had a fence around his property. Fences are good because they keep people out, but also provide very much needed cover. Larry, Carlos, and Mario were going to have to take out any soldiers that were on duty when we hit. I could trust them. If we did this right, we would not be suspected of anything. So now it seemed I was writing real-life scripts that would outdo anything you might see at the local cinema. Maybe I should add screenwriter to that resume of mine.

This is going to be big - very big, We would have to lay low after this and to see what happened. There would be high risk involved; but after all, my entire life up to that point was all about risk. Big risk. Risk that, when you lose, you die from.

I went to a gun show in Orlando and picked up three .22 pistols, and two .22 rifles. Certain materials are a little hard to find, like the brass and stainless steel screening I needed for the inside of the silencer. But I was able to get everything. For the silencer, I used a plumbing pipe for the body, which would slip over the barrel of the pistol. I had to drill and tap parts to make it all work. The first one I made was on one of the rifles. It was so silent that all you could hear was the mechanical clicking sounds, and the sound of the bullet ricocheting. Too bad the bullet went sideways because I did not line up the holes correctly. But at least I knew this is going to work as I was able to make a couple of really dependable silencer-equipped pieces. All I need for the hit now was a date and time, and I would have Mario get me a stolen car.

Then phone rang. Shit, it was Joey. He was talking fast.

"Next Wednesday, I am coming down to Carmine's house and we are going to round everybody up that was there at the rip-off and all take a polygraph," he said. "Make sure you and Lisa are in town. If you pass the polygraph, and I truly hope you do, I will need you to hang around in case someone fails the test. Then you know what to do"

"OK Joey, just give me a call", I said. My heart was pounding a mile a minute.

It was time to make our move. I called a meeting with my crew. We were going to go at night. Larry and the guys would do their work using night vision, and with total silence, just like they did in Vietnam, using knives, or maybe a good baseball bat.

First, they would secure the perimeter. Then I will go in with Lisa and take care of business. Lisa insisted that she come with me. It was against my better judgment, and my guys did not like the idea, but what the hell. Lisa was a pretty hard lady and had been through a lot.

We were going to get married, and I figured she could never testify against me, so I gave in. We got a motel room close by to gear up and get smashed. Need a good coke head to pull this off! Lisa looked hot in her vest and shoulder rig.

The night of the hit I looked like a maniac for sure. I had on my disguise, a bullet-proof vest, my 9mm for back up, and extra 9mm clips taped to the vest. All the bullets were hollow point. I was ready. There was no turning back now.

We drove past Carmine's house and kept the lights off when we opened the doors. The guys got out to take up positions and scope it out. There were only a couple of guys patrolling his grounds. That is good news for us but bad news for them.

I saw Larry hide behind a tree. When one of Carmine's guys walked past, Larry simultaneously put his hand over the guys mouth, and plunged his hunting knife into the guy a few times as he dropped lifeless to the ground.

Mario was closest to the other guy, who was smoking a cigarette by the pool. When he walked away from the pool, he would be dusted. There were a lot of trees around, which made for the greatest cover. Mario always got a kick out of hand-to-hand combat, from being in Vietnam. He said he would like to use a garrote, one of those wire things you put around someone else's neck as you squeeze the life out of them. And that is exactly what he did.

Now it's my turn to go in with Lisa. I rang the front door.

"Who the fuck is it?" Carmine yells out.

"It's me, Sal, I need to talk to you. Open the damn door, it's gonna rain."

Carmine opens the door and he asks when did I grow the beard as I pumped six bullets into him. He drops like a ton of bricks.

I hear a broad yell to Carmine, "Who is there?"

Shit, I thought. I didn't expect anybody to be there. We did not see any extra vehicles that shouldn't be there. We couldn't have any eyewitnesses. Lisa was already on her way to confront her in the living room. We could not have any more eyewitness, or so I thought.

We couldn't sanitize the scene as we had to get the hell out of here fast. No fingerprints because we wore these damn latex gloves that kept slipping off. I took the guns out to the Everglades and threw them into a canal. Good, no evidence, no eyewitness. The broad was in the wrong place at the wrong time.

The plan was to meet up in a safe house we had set up in Pittsfield, Mass., which was a very nice place to lay low. I was heading up there with Lisa and would meet the guys there in a few days. While in Carmine's house, I grabbed some cash he had lying around in his bedroom. Seemingly everything went off without a hitch. Sure, there were a few unexpected things; but that's normal when you're dealing with drugs and murder.

The next day a friend of Carmine's stopped by his house and discovered the bodies all over the place. That night it was all over the TV news, and in all the newspapers. They called it a mob hit. The state attorney gave a press conference promising to bring the perpetrators to justice.

Some people are not going to be happy with this, but they don't want to be part of a war either. When I got the call from Joey, I had to act like I was in shock, as if who would do such a thing? You see part of being a bad guy is being able to lie well, almost like being an actor. In fact, I think most of us bad guys could teach those actors a few things about acting. You see we're not doing it for fun; our lives depend on it sometimes.

Joey said that he is very uptight, that he hopes he is not next. I told him that when we find out who did this, I would take care of him free of charge. I hoped it sounded convincing.

Time to head up to Pittsfield. I needed a Lude badly.

CHAPTER EIGHT

Betrayed: The Beginning Of The End

From the beginning of time it seems that our mindless attraction to the opposite sex seems to always land us in trouble. Adam had his Eve. Samson had his Delilah. I had my Lisa. Things were about to head in a direction that I never saw coming.

Lisa and I arrived at the safe house on a beautiful spring day. The beauty of the day was overshadowed by our arguing. I noticed increasing tension between us, and I didn't know why. My guys were already there, getting the place operational.

"Sal, how ya doin, goombah? Relax and smoke a joint with us," Jimmy said, as he lit up a fat one. "The word on the street is that it was a wise guy hit. Nobody knows who done it." "Yeah, I read in the Sun Sentinel that the Bulls have no clues, no prints, no weapons, no witnesses, just bullets and casings," I said.

Lisa asked for some blow. I think to myself that she has been going overboard on Ludes and blow lately. Maybe the hit was too much for her to stomach, could have been a big mistake letting her come with me, but too late for that now.

"So what's the plan?" Mario asks.

"We do our thing. We unload what we have, but not in New York. Everybody else is lying low, so we act like we are doing the same. Keep your eyes open, and no big spending, it will attract attention," I told them.

A few days later Lisa tells me that her Mom is ill and needs to go back to Florida to see her. I offer to come along, but she says that her Mom never liked that she was hanging with a cracker. Her mom was old school.

We spoke on the phone several times. I was getting this feeling that things were breaking down a bit between us. You know that feeling when things aren't feeling right with your lady.

Several weeks had passed. I get a call from Lisa.

"Honey, I want you to come down to Florida and I want us to get married, for real."

"Really, you know I would marry you in a New York minute. Are you sure?" I replied.

"Yes, I think it's time. We can finally have kids and have a family"

"What about your Mom?" I asked, knowing that she could be a problem. "I know your Dad is cool, but she hates me."

"Mom will get used to the idea. Besides, she ain't long for this world."

So I tell the guys that I am going to go to Florida to marry Lisa, and then head back to Pittsfield. No big wedding. I am surprised by the call, but I really loved this chick. I was happy, maybe I could get out of this life and have a family, make some kids and stuff. Do some of those things my folks always wished I would. My guys had broads, but I would be the first to get hitched. We would have some fucking celebration when I got back in town with my new bride. I was to drive down in my Eldorado and meet her at the Pompano Harness Track. We had nice Box Seats. It was like a little apartment. We hardly ever used it, but we often lent it to our associates. There was a rest area on the Florida Turnpike that I stopped at and called Lisa.

"Hi Honey, I am about an hour away, can't wait to hold you in my arms."

"Sal, I can't wait to see you, and we are going to have some crazy and wild sex tonight, for sure."

Lisa knew I loved crazy and wild sex. Oh yeah! She was baiting me with the promise of sex. Now I felt a second wind. I was on my way to change my life, but too bad I didn't know in what direction.

I arrived at the track feeling like a million bucks. All I had to do was go upstairs, check in with the security, and go see my girl. There's the security booth, what a bunch of assholes. They couldn't become cops, so they became security guys. Big fucking deal.

"My name is Sal Luzani, I am in Box 420, my girl should be there now waiting for me," I said with a big smile.

"Do you have any ID?" says fat boy.

First time they ever asked for ID, I thought to myself. So I pull out my driver's license, and I see this guy give the nod to somebody. I immediately knew this ain't good. I feel the cold hard steel of a gun barrel pressing against the back of my head. At the same exact time, the guard in front of me raises up a .38 caliber and points it at my face. I could actually see the tips of the bullets in his gun, and I wanted no part of them.

A cop approached from my left, and another from my right side with guns drawn.

"Don't fucking move, Luzani, it will be your last move," says the guard who asked for the ID. Good thing I wasn't packing heat tonight.

"What the fuck is going on," I yelled.

"Mr. Luzani, you are under arrest for the murders of Carmine Esposito and Maria DeLuca." He held the indictments in his hand. Next came the Miranda Rights. They thought I would be armed, and probably would have loved to Ice me and save the taxpayers money.

I was in shock, really in shock. Did you ever have one of those moments where it felt like your heart skipped a beat? I felt like I could collapse, but gotta be strong. Obvious to me that this was a set up, but by who? I was cuffed and brought down to the Broward County Sheriff's Office. They brought me into a little interrogation room. This should be fun.

"Salvatore, you are in big trouble. You could get the chair for this. Work with us and we will guarantee you don't fry," said Captain Marcus. "If you wanna be a prick, you will be sorry." "Yeah, your old lady likes my prick," I blurted out without thinking.

He backhands me in the face, and I fall off the chair onto the floor. His partner makes like he is holding Captain Marcus back, and tells me to get up, and get back in the chair. Here we go with the good cop/bad cop show. Now, Mr. Good Cop wants me to sign a confession, to admit to two counts of first-degree murder.

"Sure thing, you want me to sign on the dotted line? Stick it up your ass," I shouted. "I demand to have a lawyer, no more bullshit."

And then I clam up.

Next I am taken to the Broward County Jail, where I am booked, fingerprinted, had my mug shots taken and was placed in a holding cell until they find a bed for me in one of the cell blocks. I knew right away that this isn't going to be over in a matter of days, but what kind of evidence could they have to make a charge like this? I would soon find out.

They wouldn't let me make a call until I got to my assigned cell, which was bullshit. I knew I was supposed to get the chance to make a call before that. They were trying to break me down. I knew all about this shit. Finally, I got to make a call after I threatened them with a civil rights lawsuit.

I called a lawyer that we had on retainer in case we got busted for anything. A professional criminal will always have a lawyer on retainer, and I mean a criminal lawyer. If he doesn't, then he's just stupid.

"Jacob, I am in the Broward County Jail Charged with two counts of first-degree murder. Get down here ASAP."

"Sal, I am already on it, you have been all over the TV news. I have copies of the indictments and will be down to the jail in the morning. Don't discuss the case with anybody," he said.

Well, I felt a little better. At least I had one of the best criminal lawyers around. Now we will find out what gives and who set me up. Finally, after four hours, I am assigned a cell. I realized that I had to watch my back in jail, can't trust anybody as this wasn't any vacation villa.

CHAPTER NINE

My New Home

So now you have a little background about how I ended up in my new home, this god forsaken jail, and how suddenly I'm a jailhouse rock star. Remember what I said back at the beginning of this book. At this point in my life things just weren't going as I had always imagined they would, and that my life was about to change forever. Well, I wasn't kidding.

So there I was sitting in jail. A caged Lion on display for the whole world to see. Everybody just kept watching the news, and then looking over at me; almost like they were trying to confirm I was the same guy.

At least they know I ain't no pussy.

The houseman, Robert, brings me to my bunk. He says all new people must take a shower, it's the rules. I say OK and hit the shower. When I get into the shower, I see Playboy photos all over the shower walls. I think what the hell are they doing there? Then I figured it out. This is the only place you get a little privacy. The photos were there for a good jerk off! I make sure I don't ever touch the walls.

That night, the place looked like a scene out of Apocalypse Now. Sheets were suspended down to separate blocks of bunks. Makeshift candles were lit and glowing in the dark. They would take thread from a sheet and wrap it around a stick and place it in a container with melted butter. Now you got a candle, and it worked pretty well. In one corner I saw two guys making toast by holding a piece of bread in a bent up wire hanger over a roll of burning toilet paper. This is nuts, I thought. I gotta get out of this place. I couldn't wait to meet up with my lawyer, Jacob.

There are a couple of Cuban guys rolling a joint. It looks like they are removing weed from a shoelace. Must have been smuggled in at a visitation. It's amazing what the bad guys can get their hands on in prison. Most people wouldn't believe it if I told them.

I go back to my bunk and lay down. I was exhausted and quickly nodded out. I am brought back to semi-consciousness by the sound of very loud, insane laughter. I open my eyes to see the face of a nut job about three inches above me. Quickly, I head-butted the nut, and grabbed his hair as I rolled out of the bed. Now I was standing, and he was kneeling down. I gave him a knee in the face and watched him fall to the ground, with a bloody nose.

The other guys yelled the guards are coming. I told the nut to get in his bunk, and keep his mouth shut if he wants to see tomorrow morning.

Lying in bed, I take a look all around me. This is surreal, like being in a movie that I can't get out of. There are 24 bunks in here, each one filled with a nut job, all innocent of course. At least I know that I am no angel.

There is one older guy that keeps on staring at me. I try to ignore him and look at a magazine, but he doesn't stop. This guy comes over to my bunk, and sits down, uninvited, which is a big "No-No" in the joint.

"Hey Buddy, I can make you feel real good tonight," he says with a big shit-eating grin on his face. "Oh yeah? How you going to do that," I ask, getting myself psyched up to strike.

"For a pack of smokes, I will give you some great head," he says.

"Oh really? let me think about that", I responded as I elbowed him in the face. He falls to the ground and spins around to attack me. By now, I am standing up, so I bob and weave, and shoot a straight jab to his mouth, followed up with an uppercut. He went out like a light. The other guys loved the show as they yelled and screamed like they were at a prize fight.

Just then a guard walks by and sees this asswipe lying on the floor, bleeding.

He gets on his two-way and calls for back-up to enter the cell.

"Luzani, what the fuck happened here?" he says.

"I will be honest captain, this moron came over and sat on my bed while I was nodding, and put his hand on my dick, so I nailed him."

"Looks like you more than nailed him, looks like you hammered him. Lucky for you we have had multiple complaints from every cell we put him in; we will get him out of here."

"Chow time. Chow time," yells a guard.

I look at the clock and see it is 5 a.m. What the fuck kind of time is 5 a.m. for breakfast? One of my new friends tells me that if I don't grab a tray, I won't be able to eat till around 11 a.m. I'd better get used to this new routine. I had been arrested before, but never held without bond. No bond on murder cases. Things should be easier now that I have kicked some ass. The rest of the inmates know not to mess with me. I hear the clanging of cell block doors opening. "Luzani, attorney visitation, up front, now," a guard said.

Thank God Jacob was finally here. I am brought down to an interview room.

Jacob shakes my hand, and whispers not to say anything, the place may be bugged. He takes out a legal pad and starts writing in very tiny letters.

"Lisa set you up," he wrote.

"No fucking way!" I yell out loud. "It can't be, she would never do that. We are going to get married."

So much for the legal pad.

Jacob says to sit down and listen.

"I know this is a shocker, but it's true," he said.

I started to squirm around in my chair.

"While you were up North, Lisa was seeing other guys in Florida. She was very high one night and told some guy that she was fucking that she took part in a double murder. The guy told her to go to the police. The next day, when she sobered up, she realized what she had done. Her dad brought her to a family lawyer, who contacted the state attorney's office. She agreed to testify against you for complete immunity from prosecution."

This is a lot to absorb all at once, I thought. So much for love. Jacob goes on to say that the state is going to ask for the electric chair and this judge will use it, if convicted. He said the state would offer a plea deal, and he is waiting to hear what they offer.

Meanwhile, he will file for discovery so we can see what the evidence is and find out what Lisa said. I am speechless. As he packs up his shit, he says,

"If you don't take a deal, you will be convicted, and you will be given the electric chair. You will be on death row for eight years, and you will be executed."

I sit there staring at the wall. I had said earlier that things were about to change forever, and they did. That turned out to be the fucking understatement of the century. It looked like the only thing I was going to be married to was ten thousand volts.

What the hell was I going to do? Gotta be strong, I thought. I heard of guys beating their cases before, but not two counts of first-degree murder. The only thing I could do was wait for arraignment tomorrow. It was turning out to be a very bad day indeed.

CHAPTER TEN

The Great Escape

In my line of work one thing that is very important is the ability to adapt quickly. So I'm in jail, and could be facing the death penalty, so what? Things are never as they seem, and life always has a way of taking unexpected twists. I just figured while I was there, I should make the best of a bad situation.

Early in the morning, after chow, names are called to line up for transfer to the courthouse. My name was called, and I was put back in cuffs, hooked to a waist-chain and leg shackles. It looks wild and is hard to walk when chained like that. We are all brought to a holding cell in back of the courtroom.

There was a great assortment of citizens in the room: murderers, rapists, armed robbers, burglars, drug dealers, homeless degenerates, and child molesters. Nice crowd. When my name is called, I stood before the judge. My attorney pleads not guilty for me.

Judge Harvey Polensky has a reputation of being quite tough on the stand. He has given out the electric chair several times and is not shy about it. My attorney, who has scared the shit out of me by now, takes me aside and says:

"Watch what you say to your cell mates. The state attorney will try to get cell mates facing a lot of time to testify against you for a reduced sentence, so think before you speak."

"Ok, but how long is this gonna take, I don't have time for this shit?"

"It will be months, so get yourself into a routine, or you will get depressed. Read books, work out, go to the law library"

"They have a law library in Jail?" I asked.

"Yes, and a damn good one. I will write several motions and keep them on their toes." I later learned the value of filing a lot of motions. The state attorney's office has a tremendous workload, not like a private attorney. Good to jam them up with motions that need a response.

This is going to be the fight of my life. Better get my act together if I am going to be the survivor that I always claimed to be. I see guys all around me that have given up. Some of them sleep all the time in a desperate attempt to escape reality. I am determined not to be one of those guys. I figure that if I am convicted, I could always find a way to escape.

Failure was not an option for me, and there was no way I'd spend the rest of my life sitting around here with all these jerkoffs playing cards and trying to figure out how to smuggle in my next drug.

After being brought back to my bunk in this dormitory type of cell, I sit and look around. I spot a pile of magazines and some books. I see guys either watching TV, sleeping, or reading. It's crazy that guys will fight over which TV show to watch. They will kill each other over phone time. The phone is brought around to each cell at a certain time. Everyone gets six minutes. You go over your six minutes, and you're on someone else's time. Good way to get an ass beating.

Days turn into weeks. I have gotten into the routine of reading books and brushing up on mathematics. I even made flash cards to study vocabulary. The books I loved to read most were about lawyers, like F. Lee Baily. My muscles are getting huge from working out almost every day.

I was feeling strong. Jacob has been taking depositions of state witnesses and filing for discovery. One day I am brought over to the holding cell by myself to attend a motion hearing. I had asked Jacob to have me brought to all hearings. I want to know everything that is happening. After the guard took my cuffs off, and closed the cell door, he left through a door that led directly to an outside corridor. I start playing with the door, and to my surprise it opens!

That's right, the freakin door slid open. That moron guard didn't slam it hard enough.

This is how your situation could change at a moment's notice, and you gotta be ready to adapt. Now it's time for a quick decision: Do I stay in the cell, or do I jump the next bailiff that comes through the door and try to escape? I walk out of the cell and do a little dance, then go back in and sit down. The decision was not to add to my charges. I would never know if I could have beaten the case. So, I left the door open and got comfortable. Corporal Escalante comes through the door.

"What the fuck is going on? Why is this door open," he asks.

"Not my fault, it was just left open," I replied.

As he closed the door he said, "Thanks Sal, we owe you one."

He knew right then and there that I could have made the choice to jump him, and get his gun and shoot him, but that wasn't the way I wanted to handle my case. At that point I felt as though I had to learn about this court process myself, if I was going to stand any chance at all of mounting a good defense. I wanted my destiny to be in my hands and not somebody else. The next time they call for law library, I will be first in line. I needed to find out what goes on in there.

The next day the call is made for the law library, and of course I'm first in line. I am brought into a large room. All the walls are lined with shelves packed with books, books, and more books. I felt pretty lost at first, but so what. This was the first time I was ever in a law library. There was a big table in one corner where a bunch of guys sat with piles of papers and books before them. I was told that these guys were the jailhouse lawyers who helped inmates with their cases. They were treated like royalty. I figured I better brush up on my chess because these guys were into chess big time. A lot of guys play chess in the joint because it's a great way to pass time and helps to keep the brain working. I would have figured that they didn't have the brains for chess, I would have been wrong.

One of the guys I often played chess with was from the Outlaw Motorcycle Gang. A very big, scary looking guy named Jake. He was in for beating some guy to death. One day he came to the law library with me and says:

"Sal, me and a few guys are going to break out of this place, you are welcome to come, either way, we could use your help."

"Holy Shit, are you kidding. I don't know if I would go but you can count on me for whatever help you need," I said, thinking this is nuts. "How you gonna escape out of this joint?"

"You see that room across the corridor, we can get into that room. We are going to climb out down onto the roof, and then down to the street where we will have a car waiting," he explained.

"But this is six floors up man, you could get killed."

"What's the difference, I would rather die trying for freedom, than sitting in here waiting to fry. We got it all planned."

He went on to explain that they were gathering a shit load of sheets and braiding them together into a rope. One of the trustees would make sure the door to the mechanical room was unlocked.

The grating over the window would be loosened and put back into place. One thing I knew for sure was that I ain't climbing down no rope from six stories above the roof. These guys are nuts. Not for me.

We would all go up to the law library on one of the allowed nights. It would be filled to the max. When we were lined up in the corridor to be brought back to the cell, I would start a fight with a child molester, because the guards hated them also, and I would get off easy. I would say it was self-defense and the other guys would back me on the story. So one night, when the guards came and got everyone out of the law library, and into this corridor, I was given the signal. I said to Jerry, the molester guy:

"Hey asshole, you like little boys, I got something for you."

I punched him in the face. Then I just started beating the shit out of him.

Everyone was screaming to kill him. Meanwhile, Jake and the two other guys made it into the mechanical room and laid low.

The guards came running in like gang busters. They ordered all of us to the floor and brought Jerry the Molester down to the infirmary. He didn't look to good. But he deserved a good beating anyway.

We are all brought back to our cells. On the way down in the elevator, one of the guys fakes a seizure. Rolando started foaming at the mouth, and shaking all over, as he laid on the elevator floor. Great acting. This was to buy some more time for the escapees. I knew all hell was about to break loose at any time now. A guard comes to the cell and says:

"Luzani, come with me, the captain wants to speak with you."

I am brought to a holding cell by the elevators. They want to know what I know about this breakout.

It is then that I learned that the rope broke and Jake broke his back. The other guys had broken ankles and one guy had a broken leg. Well, I guess I made the right decision.

"No shit," I said. "Well that was a stupid thing to do. Who the hell would attempt to climb down a rope from the sixth floor?"

"How did you know it was from the sixth floor," he asks.

"I heard the guards talking on the way to see you. No kidding, I had nothing to do with this"

"What about the fight? Was that just a cover?" he asks.

"Hell no, that asshole said something to one of the guys about licking his kid brother He had it coming to him, sir."

"I will check out your story and it better check out or you are going to solitary, Luzani."

Well, this blew over and I did not have to go to solitary. Too many other cell mates backed up my story. Weeks turn into months. My case is getting close to trial. One day Jacob gives me book to read by F. Lee Baily. Wow, this should be a great read. I loved his books. One thing in this book catches my eye, F. Lee says:

"It doesn't matter whether you are innocent or guilty. It is if the jury believes what you tell them." I read this over, and over.

Now I have some hope. I will take the stand and convince them I am not guilty. Maybe I can beat this case. I have to just convince 12 people that I am not a murderer. That should be easy, right?

The next meeting with my attorney is a stunner. He tells me that there are two cell mates who will testify against me. He says that the State Attorney's Office has offered a deal.

I plead guilty to both counts and get seven years on each. That's 14 years. No electric chair. If I don't cop a plea, they will ask for the chair.

Jacob wants me to take the deal and a lot is at stake. I tell him that if I take the deal, I will never know if I could have walked. He says that Lisa is going to testify that she saw me build the silencers and kill the two victims.

"The jury will believe her story and you will be convicted and sentenced to the electric chair," he says once again.

I could never figure out why he kept saying that to me, maybe to make himself feel better about representing me?

No Deal. We will come up with a defense. I could see that legal mind of Jacobs working overtime. This guy is supposed to be so damn great, let him come up with a defense. It was time for him to prove himself.

"Say the girl did it, and you backed out at the last minute. Admit to the rip-off, but not the murders.

You will be admitting to a crime, and it will give you more credibility."

I like this idea, it made sense. Maybe we can pull this off after all.

The trial is fast approaching. I start practicing my facial expressions as I gaze into the mirror. I have to know what my facial expressions look like at all times. Jacob says I need to come off meek and timid or we will lose. This will be the most important day of my life. I wanted to make sure I was ready.

I better be perfect on the stand. Jacob says we will get last closing argument if we don't call any witnesses, just me.

Jury selection begins. One of my cell mates lets me borrow his pin striped suit. I look like a freakin lawyer. The

Trial will start after we pick a jury. It took two weeks to seat a jury.

We felt it was a good jury. Too bad I couldn't buy them off.

The first day of the trial I am brought to one of the three holding cells behind the courtroom. In the next cell is one of the guys who flipped against me. He says he is sorry, but they made him.

I say: "Great, fuck you, too. Payback is a bitch. you are now a marked man."

The state called 15 witnesses. The gun dealer that sold me the guns couldn't even ID me as I sat in my nice clean crisp new suit. Other witnesses like the motel clerk, pointed right at me.

"Yes, he is the one," they said.

Another cell mate testified that I confessed the crime to him. Jacob cut him to pieces on cross examination. When Lisa testified, she said she saw me do it all. Jacob got her to sound like an overbearing, maniacal broad.

This was getting really good. I felt like I was in an old Perry Mason movie. At the close of the state's case, my attorney announced that we are not calling any witnesses, and that Salvatore Luzani will take the stand. The state flips out and asks for a delay. My attorney had filed a false witness list to throw them off and lead them into thinking we had a different defense. The state thought we were going to place the blame on a rival criminal gang. Now this is getting even more interesting.

I was on the stand for four hours. I would let my voice trail off so the state attorney had to ask the judge to tell me to speak up. I came off like a real wimp. The state attorney kept hammering away at me, trying to catch me up in a lie. But I was way too smart and way too cool for that. The jury looks like they are buying my rap. The jury deliberated for days. I discovered that one of the holding cells backed up to the bathroom in the jury room.

I knew so because I could hear a toilet flushing. When I put my ear against the wall, I could hear the jury arguing over the case, as long as the bathroom door wasn't closed. Well, this is unreal. Did you ever hear of such a thing? I heard them say:

"If it isn't first degree than what is it?"

"The girl did it... he couldn't do such a thing; he is a wimp." When I told Jacob what I heard, he said not to tell him anymore, he wanted to be surprised.

I was feeling pretty damn good but didn't say a word to anybody. The next day, I was brought before the judge for the reading of the verdict. The court was packed with standing room only. Newspapers and TV news crews were there with cameras flashing. It was like I had become a celebrity or something.

"Mr. Luzani, please rise," says Judge Asshole.

He asks the Jury Foreman: "Has the jury reached a verdict?"

"Yes, your Honor."

"Please read the verdict."

"We the people of Broward County Florida, as to count one of the indictment, first degree murder, find the defendant not guilty, as to count two of the indictment, first-degree murder, not guilty, so say we all."

I am about to shit in my drawers. Is this for real? Have I just been found not guilty? For real? Is this nightmare finally coming to an end?

Jacob puts his arm around me and says:

"We did it, you beat one of the hardest of all cases to beat, this case will make my career."

The judge asks the jury if they have any questions. And he says:

"Salvatore Luzani, you have been found not guilty by a jury of your peers. You are free to go."

Again, this wasn't the way I thought things would go, but this time I was happy to be wrong.

Jacob escorts me out of the courtroom as news reporters are snapping pictures and shouting questions to me.

"Sal, what are your plans?"

"I just want to get on with the rest of my life," I said in my best innocent-man voice. He brings me back to the jail to get my belongings and return the suit. Everybody is happy for me. They wish me good luck. I go downstairs and I am given an ID card, because I had no identification.

Then Jacob brings me to his office. This whole thing took eight months and it was the longest eight months of my life. I can't believe this. I am free.

I get a call from Lisa.

"You know you killed them, why did you say I did it? I thought you loved me."

"I loved you until you turned into a piece of shit," I said.

It was obvious she was on a tapped phone, probably sitting in the state attorney's office. You should have seen their faces when the not guilty verdict was read. They were not happy. Jacob calls me the next morning and tells me to leave town quickly. The state attorney is going to charge me for the armed robbery I admitted to during the trial. That was the chance we took. But we beat the murder charges, so I couldn't complain.

My friend gave me his car and all the money in his pocket. I hit the road, with the intention of not stopping until I got out of Florida.

Now I am a wanted man, on the run, but as far as I was concerned. I had another pretty good day.

CHAPTER ELEVEN

Wanted By the FBI

On the run again. My plan is to drive all night until I get to Georgia, then I will get a room in some flea bag motel. Got to keep a low profile; go over my options. I always wondered what it would be like to be on the run, now I will find out. I understand from Jacob that I am on the FBI Most Wanted List — Armed and Dangerous. Boy, I would like to see that poster, maybe I could have it framed. As I drive, I am realizing certain facts.

The FBI will monitor any known associates, friends, and family. Contacting my people will place them in jeopardy and they could be charged with any of several felonies. When I get further north, I will contact one of the guys, and make a meeting somewhere safe. I need some cash, some weed, and a piece.

I will have to find some place to go where I can get a new ID. I once read in a book the best way to get new ID, and not phony ID. Now we will see if it works, or if it was all bullshit. I will pick up an almanac, and find a city to head for, that fits what the book said. Not too big a city, not too small either.

When I finally got out of Florida, I got a room in a flea bag motel. Old furniture, black & white TV, lousy bed. I better get used to this. I don't want to go back to jail, I hated it, no chicks.

There was weed there though, really good weed, but I would rather not go back for sure. After I made a pit stop in my room, I went to the convenience store across the street. Try to act normal, not like someone on the run. As I am selecting some goodies to bring back to my room, I hear a voice:

"Freeze, you're under arrest."

My heart stopped for a second. I thought this is it, already? As I turn around, and to my surprise, I see it is two kids playing around with toy guns; goofing around with each other! What a fucking relief. I am sure I turned three shades of white. I looked away and took several deep breaths. Got to get out of here. I pay for the almanac and head back to the room.

Well, it looks like Springfield, Mass. is where I am headed. The population is about 350,000, not too big, not too small. I travel as many back roads as possible. In North Carolina, I came up to a police roadblock. They are standing there checking vehicles. They have rifles. Is this for me? Too late to do anything about it.

I will try to act normal. I roll down my window, and say:

"Hello Officer, what's going on?"

"Several convicts escaped from the county jail, we are checking all vehicles, please exit the vehicle."

"Sure, and I hope you catch the bastards."

I get out and he looks around and asks me to open the trunk. Then, I am on my way.

Wow, that was a close one. This is going to be a real trip if you know what I mean.

I stop in Maryland and meet up with Mario. He has my old 9mm from the Pittsfield safe house. He also has weed, coke, and five grand in cash. He is the best. I will make it up to him. I head for Springfield, Mass. I will make a phony ID using a portion of the alien address card from the post office. I have done this before.

You put your picture and a fingerprint on the backside, then laminate it with that plastic shit. I will need this to pull off what I have in mind. First, I will need a base to operate out of for maybe a couple of weeks. I came across a motor court type of place. Little shit cottages, should be fine. I go in to register, and they couldn't give a shit if I was a mass murderer. Good. Now I have an address to receive mail. Time to head down to city hall. I tell them that I am doing bio-statistical research and that I want to see the records of children who died before the age of six. They buy it and take me to a room where there are these big ledger type books. Death Records. I write down eight male children who died at an early age. They never had a Social Security Card, never had any credit. So far, so very good. I then leave and get some money orders. I am going to try to get copies of the birth certificates. I figured that one department would not know what the other was doing. All I could do now is wait. I bought some dumbbells so I could work out. I ended up dropping one and broke my big toe.

I went to an emergency room where they put a cast on my foot. This is great, now what? After a few days, I tried to remove the cast by soaking it in the bathtub. Dumb idea, it didn't work. Now I really had to get this cast off. I got a hold of a pair of pliers and broke it off, piece by piece.

I waited and waited. Finally, I received a total of three birth certificates. I guess the book, was a good book. Next I was able to acquire Social Security Numbers. I told them my parents were rich, and I never needed one. Soon, I had three social security numbers. Now I need drivers licenses.

I blow this dump and head for Bennington, Vt. I hear it is a beautiful place. I got a room in a motel up in the mountains. I arranged for a driver's test. The inspector asked me why I never had a driver's license. I gave him the same line that my parents were rich and I was chauffeured everywhere. Soon, I had three drivers licenses with different names.

Now I am feeling cool. Next I apply for credit cards. Let's see if I get credit cards, after all, these names do not have tarnished credit.

I need a way to bring in money. There was a nearby Kmart, where I bought a cheapo suit and some phony gold jewelry. Now I looked like a businessman. My idea was to rent IBM Selectric Typewriters in one state and sell them in another. I would have at least 30 days before they even knew what's up. After renting a few machines, I headed for upstate New York.

It was night, and I was tired. I stopped at a motel on the interstate. Inside my room, I removed the serial number plates and use plastic model putty to fill the holes. Then I painted them to match the rest of the machine. They looked great. I placed ads in some flyers.

When I got up in the morning, I go down to the restaurant to have some chow. The place is full of state troopers eating breakfast. I guess I will get it to go!

When I went outside to get something from my car, I see that across the street is the state trooper barracks. What a great choice of motels. I got to get out of here pronto, but I have ads coming out with this phone number. So I lay low and use room service often. I got some calls and sold the machines for a good price pretty easily. I do this scenario several times.

Rent in one state, sell in another. Soon I figured that I overstayed my welcome. It was time to move on. I hear from friends that the FBI visited them. They are getting closer. It is off to Hartford, Conn., where I will set up shop. I was able to get an apartment but had no furniture. I went to a furniture rental store and rented stuff to fill up my new pad. Now, I thought it would be a good time to find a hooker for some sex. I was pretty horny by now. I brought back a black chick who gave me a blow job in return for some blow. Get it? A blow job for some blow! Funny, I thought.

I looked in the classifieds and decided to try to get a job. I saw an ad from Rollins Security. I went down the next day and had an interview.

They liked me and said I would have to pass a background check. I ended up getting the job. They gave me a company car to drive and sent me for training. What a bunch of morons. It was really a telephone sales job. Getting appointments from calling cold to the phone book. It sucked, I didn't want to work for anyone for peanuts. I had to get some kind of a scam going so I can afford a good lifestyle.

I ended up securing two credit cards which I retrieved from a P.O. Box that I had set up. I went crazy in Hartford charging the cards to the max, buying all kinds of shit, especially gold items. I figured I could always get rid of gold. I bought some great clothes and I was looking good.

Next I headed for Liberty, New York, where I put down a deposit on a new Jeep Wagoner, and two snow mobiles. I was buying one for Mario, he dug them. I met with a real estate broker who showed me a small old house on sixteen acres for a very cheap price. It was out in the sticks. Perfect. I gave him a security deposit and signed the lease. It is hard to remember who I am supposed to be, not used to being called by other names.

Things were looking up for a change. The morning after I signed the lease, I went to town and open up a bank account. I had to have checks so I could pay the utilities and eventually burn out.

After I opened the account, I headed back to my hide out. Soon, I realized I left my wallet at the bank. This is very, very bad. How could I have done this? All of my three ID's were in the wallet, along with the credit cards and Social Security cards. I could not do anything without them. This sucks.

I call the bank and a guy who says he is the manager has my wallet and says that I could pick it up any time I want. OK, I tell him I will be right there. I thought very hard and deep about what to do. I knew that there was a good chance I will be arrested at the bank, but I had no choice, as I could not go through all of this again.

I made a call to Mario and told him to go to my hide out and take whatever he wanted. It was loaded with merchandise from the credit card purchases in Connecticut. I told him the story, and he said good luck. I would need a lot of luck. When I arrived at the bank, everything looked normal. I go inside and spot the managers desk. He looks OK, so I head over to his desk. I said my name is Charles Anthony, and I left my wallet here. He tells me to sit down.

"Mr. Anthony, I am with the Liberty Police Department, we believe you are attempting to commit some kind of fraud on this bank. You need to come down to the station to answer some questions. Will you come peacefully, or do we have to put the cuffs on?" he said.

"Am I under arrest?" I asked.

"No, but if you don't come with me, you will be."

Well, this is not going to be a very nice day, I thought to myself. So the jig is up and I agree to come down to the station. He brings me to the back of the bank, and places me in a police car. Now, I am thinking what the heck am I going to do? I had to go back to the bank, I could not go on without my wallet, simple as that. We get to the station, and I am brought into an office near the front door.

They want to know why I have three sets of ID. I tell them I am in the security business, and I can't use my real name as doing so would compromise my clients safety. They thought that sounded good, but they wanted to know why I did not have any business cards, no fliers, and no catalogs. Nothing to support my claim.

So now they are pissed off, and tell me to undress completely, and bend over and crack a smile. I have done this many times in jail, so I am used to this. They are trying to break me down. It won't work. They say they will be back after they run a check on me for warrants. A half hour turns into an hour. Here I am, ten feet from the front door, nobody around. I get up and walk out the door.

I head across the parking lot, and down the street. I hear a door open, and a cop yells out:

"Keep walking and you're a dead man."

"Then place me under arrest, or you can shoot someone with no charges," I yell back as I stand my ground.

"OK, asshole, you're under arrest," he yells back.

"For what?" I say, as I walk back to the police station.

"Well, let's start with bank fraud, attempted escape," he said.

"I'm sure we could add a few charges," he blurts out at me.

"OK, OK. I get the picture, but you guys never came back. I wasn't even under arrest," I said with a smirk.

"Well, you have a lot of balls, I'll say that much for you."

He grabbed me under the arm, and briskly ushered me back into an interrogation room. I wasn't going to try that again, that was for sure. He said they are waiting for the Teletype to print out any warrants that I may have outstanding.

I thought for a long while, and I came to the conclusion that this was the end of the trail. I could not go anywhere without my wallet. It was only a matter of time before my FBI warrant came up with the armed robbery charges.

I was sick and tired of being on the run. Not fun anymore. I decided to tell them about the warrant.

"Officer, can I speak with you," I said through the door.

When he came in I told him that I was wanted in Florida on armed robbery charges, and that there was a federal warrant on me for interstate flight. He smiled broadly.

"Well, imagine that. I knew there was something wrong here, with all those IDs," he said.

All of a sudden they are all nice to me. They have a great arrest to brag about. It will look good for them. I am no petty thief.

Now I will have to decide if I will waive extradition back to Florida, or if I stay here and fight whatever charges these guys come up with.

They put me in a van and take me to the Monticello County Jail. By now, they all know I beat two murder charges. They all look at me like I am a mass murderer. I end up in a cell with about twelve guys, mostly local schmucks. At least I get my own little cell. I do incline push-ups with my feet on the sink. Gotta keep in shape. I do squats holding on to the bars. In the next cell is a Chinese guy who was brought in from assaulting somebody in the hotel where he works in the kitchen.

This nut job is making his sink overflow, and his cell is loaded with water. He is stomping around, splashing in the water, and muttering crazy things. He comes close by my cell and says in a low, insane tone:

"I am here now, fuck you all. I will show all of you who I am."

"That's great, now go to fucking sleep and sober up," I said. The guards ran in and brought him out to a dry cell. They knew there was something wrong with this guy. The next day, we are all in the common area, which was like a corridor that passed by the front of all the cells. When they opened the doors, we could come out and walk back and forth. Mr. Nut Job slowly walks up to each and every guy and makes these mock karate gestures at them.

No telling when he may decide to actually strike somebody. Now it's my turn. He comes up to me, about two feet in front of me, and starts making Bruce Lee sounds and doing some moves. We are both staring at each other intently, but I am aware of his every movement. There was no doubt in my mind that this guy is going to strike. At the right time, I lunge and grab him by the throat, and I squeeze. At the same time, I smash his head against the bars.

I see blood coming out of his scalp. I must have split his fucking head open. I guess he picked the wrong guy to fuck with. Not his day. I am OK, not a mark on me, just some blood to wash off. All that karate stuff is great, but not if the other guy gets the first shot. I always get the first shot.

The guards came and took this guy to the Hospital. They locked me in my cell and said there would be extra charges for this. They interviewed all the other guys who backed me up. I had no choice. When the cops came back to talk to me, we worked out a deal. I would waive extradition to Florida, plead guilty to a misdemeanor for the false ID, and they would drop all other charges. I would get time served. Now, all I could do is wait to be transported by air marshals back to Florida. I had heard about this, but never actually had to be transported as a prisoner. This should be an experience I will always remember.

CHAPTER TWELVE

The Long Journey Through Our Criminal Justice System And Beyond!

I was beginning to feel like a very important bad guy. Was this how the rest of my life was going to be, I thought? It seems that once you're on the radar, there's no getting off. "Luzani, get your shit you're flying today," Officer Jackass yells. I've gotten used to hearing this stuff. Well, all I own could fit into a paper bag.

"Let's get the show on the road," I said, thinking about the trip back to Florida.

Soon, I was placed in a police van, and brought to the local county airport.

There on the runway, was a small, twin engine aircraft. Shit, I hate small planes. Ever fly on a small plane? They are all over the place. The wind knocks them side to side.

I was driven right out onto the runway, next to the plane. I see two other convicts already on board. It turns out that these air marshals fly around picking convicts up for transport to their new homes, or prisons. One of the marshals places leg chains on me, and a waist-chain. My handcuffs are then connected to the waist chain. I am seated in the toy plane, and my leg chains are locked to the back of the co-pilot's seat. If this thing goes down, we don't stand a chance.

We all give each other the nod and find out our points of origin. I was the only one from this upstate New York area. All of us were headed for Lake Butler Reception Center in Florida. We would lay over one night when we pick up the last guy around the half-way point.

At one gas stop, I had to take a leak. They attached a leash-like chain to my waist-chain and lead me to a tree. If I wanted to take a leak, I would have to do it in the open, like a dog. So I did.

These marshal guys were all business, but they were not bastards. In a few hours we would be seeing our destination. I keep thinking to myself that this is all wrong, what have I done to my life that I am chained up in a prison plane? Off in a distance, I could see what looked like a row of lights delineating a crude runway, then there were two rows of lights.

As we swooped down out of the night sky, I could see that the lights were actually kerosene torches. Holy shit! This is like right out of a movie. I would be transferred onto another plane and flown to Fort Lauderdale. When we arrived back at the Broward County Detention Center, all the guards remembered me:

"Hey Sal, you couldn't stay away from us."

"We missed you; we'll find you a great cell, don't worry, we won't put you in with the gladiators."

"Thanks, I appreciate that." Gladiators referred to the young guys. They fight all the time, over anything. I would rather be in a cell with the older guys.

I went to court the next day for arraignment on armed robbery charges. A public defender was appointed. I plead not guilty. No bond. My last attorney cost over $60,000, and my funds were pretty much a thing of the past. This young public defender wasn't going to determine my future if I could help it. I figured I need to get to the law library and see what I could learn. There must be something I could do about getting a better lawyer.

Some of the jailhouse lawyers remembered me and called me over.

"Sal, you back in town?"

"Yeah, and I have armed robbery charges, and they will throw the book at me."

"You got a public defender, or a private lawyer?"

I told him that I had a public defender, and is there anything I could do? He said he could help. I would have to learn about filing a US Code 42, Section 1983 Civil Rights Lawsuit. Oh, is that all? What the fuck was he talking about? First, I would have to file a suit against the public defender's office.

This would create a conflict of interests. Then I file the federal civil rights lawsuit, and they order the judge to appoint a private attorney. This was done before, a couple of years ago. We talked a while, and I thanked him. Next, I started walking around the law library, studying each section.

Then it came to me, all of a sudden, I realized this is nothing more than a reference library. I taught myself how to look up key words and find the corresponding cases.

I sat with a Black's Law Dictionary, and looked up everything I didn't understand, which was just about everything. I came to the law library as often as I was permitted. I was filling up legal pads one after the other. I was loving the fact that I was beginning to get the picture.

I was absorbing this shit like a sponge. Who knew? I had copies of all my attorney's past motions from the first case. One of the jailhouse lawyers told me that all I have to do to file a motion is to use the same format and make some changes. Cool, I could handle that. Then I would give it to a guard, who brought these motions and pleadings to the court clerk, and the judge would schedule a hearing. I hand wrote on my little old legal pad a civil suit against the Broward County Public Defender's Office for a number of counts.

First, I stated that I was being denied due process and their caseload and lack of communications with me violated my Constitutional Rights. It really didn't matter what I said, just the filing of the suit set up the conflict of interests. They could no longer represent me. After the lawsuit was filed, I filled out Federal Forms for the US Code 42 Lawsuit and filed it for free. I was ruled indigent because I had no money.

It took months, but one day I got a letter from the federal court. I was granted a court order demanding that the judge appoint private counsel. Now, I am feeling good! I drafted a motion to appoint private counsel, and I gave a list of five criminal attorneys who were all famous. I would be happy with any of them. I was brought to court one early morning.

"Well, Mr. Luzani, I see that you have been keeping busy in the law library," the judge said.

"Yes, your Honor, I am trying to better myself."

"I am going to appoint Mr. Charles Flanagan to represent you on these current charges.

Is that acceptable to you, Mr Luzani?"

"Yes, your honor. Thank you very much."

Man did I feel good inside. I learned to speak loud and clear. To articulate every word. I liked this lawyer stuff. I found that I could stand my own ground in court. I understood almost everything. I would object when the state attorney tried to pull some shit. I was feeling empowered.

The judge appointed the first guy on my list, who was a high-priced attorney, for free! Word got around quick back at the jail that I had won my motion.

The next time I went to the law library, I was invited to sit with the jailhouse lawyers at the big table in the corner. I was one of them now. As the weeks went by, I studied this shit every day. I started writing motions for the other inmates. One guy said he was freaking out in his head because he couldn't get his medication. I wrote a Petition for a Writ of Habeas Corpus for him and he was taken before the judge. The jail was ordered to medicate the guy. Word was getting around that I was the man to see for help on your case. Before long, guards were bringing guys to my cell from all over the jail. It was like my cell was my office. I even had guards that were taking criminal justice courses at college come to me and ask me questions. I was getting cases dismissed on technicalities, like the 21-day rule, where the state has 21 days to file charges or they had to let the guy go home. Some guys I had gotten out more than once.

I needed to see a dentist for a filling. The jail only pulls teeth, no fillings. I filed a motion to see a dentist with the court clerk. I was brought to court, and the judge granted my motion, and signed the court order prepared by me. I learned how to prepare court orders by studying my attorney's work. It is always better if you prepare the court's order, otherwise your adversary, who just lost, will have to prepare it. Dig?

So, one day the guards come and get me to go to the dentist. They place me in leg chains and handcuffs connected to a waist-chain. When they march me into the reception area at the dentist, the patients sitting there almost fainted. After that, I was asked not to return, which I could understand.

On the way back to the jail, Officer Mendez asks me if I want some Burger King. This is a real "No-No" for a corrections officer to do while transporting a prisoner. It means he has to open the car door and hand me something, then open it again to retrieve the trash. He will be taking a big chance. Well, I am shocked, and I say that would be like a dream come true, but he doesn't have to do it.

He says, "Remember when the cell door was left open at your murder trial?, and you decided not to make a break for it, well this is a little thanks for making a decent decision back then." So he stopped at a Burger King and got me a bunch of stuff. We ate the stuff on the way back to the jail, and he stopped to throw everything away. I thanked him profusely.

Rolando Martinez was brought to my cell in the middle of the night. He needed some real help. It would be his third fall and he faced a career criminal charge. He had a public defender, and knew he was doomed. I told him I had a risky plan. If it worked, it would be cool as hell. This was never done before and would be a one-time winner. I had drawn up a certificate of service that listed all the motions the guard would bring to the court. I made sure I had a large number of motions and listed a motion for speedy trial for Rolando.

This meant that the State had sixty days to go to trial, or the case must be dismissed. The only catch was that there was *no motion* for speedy trial in the bunch. I knew the guard wouldn't check because he didn't give a shit what he was bringing to the court, but he was always willing to sign off on it. Now, all we had to do is wait. Next on my list was to file a suit against the jail for overcrowding, and denial of Constitutional Rights. Soon, I filed another federal suit against the department of corrections for inadequate medical care.

I was now a high-profile jailhouse lawyer. I had ordered and received little labels that stated I was a legal advocate. I placed them on all the motions I wrote. The guys I learned from were now asking me questions. When I would get a guy out, he would put money in my commissary account to pay his respects. I was living it up. I had my own radio, and plenty of goodies to stuff my face with.

I got this idea to write a thesis, it would be "On Crime, Justice, Prevention, and The Law." I made up forms to use to interview prisoners. I would ask them all the same questions, such as what influence drugs and/or booze had on their case. Guards were bringing guys to the law library so that I could interview them. I placed copies of my best handwritten motions, as well as court orders into this treatise thing I was writing. I ended up with a 100 page paper, documenting some of my experiences as a jailhouse lawyer.

A local radio personality, known as Skipper Chuck, came to the jail and interviewed me for a radio show about my suit against the jail for overcrowding. He tried to make me look like some dumb convict, but I held my own. He kept asking me if I was qualified to practice law.

I kept responding, "Why don't you ask some of the guys who are now free thanks to me?"

One day, Officer Rico comes up to my cell door.

"Hey Sal, the Warden wants to have a private meeting with you."

"What for? I didn't do anything."

"You'll find out, let's go, now!"

Well, I wondered what is going on here. Are they going to take me somewhere and beat the shit out of me? I am ushered into the warden's plush office.

"Sal, have a seat. Let's have a little talk. Sure nice to meet you in person. You have been very active in the law library filing all kinds of lawsuits against the Department of Corrections, and everybody else. I hear attorneys and judges joking about your legal exploits in the cafeteria. You have made quite a name for yourself; you should have become a lawyer. Sal, you are driving me crazy. What's it gonna take to leave us alone?"

Wow, the Warden is asking me to back off. I think for a moment. I have to be careful; I don't want it to get around that I am cooperating with the warden. That could be a death sentence.

"Sorry to be such a pain in the ass, but I try to keep busy, I said. "I tell you what, with all due respect, are you willing to make a deal?"

"What have you got in mind," he said.

"I will stop filing any actions against the jail, and I will let the other actions fade away. All I ask is to be able to go to the gym, or the law library whenever I want to, within reason," I said, thinking this is a trip!

He thought about it for a moment.

"We can do that, but I expect you to back off like you promised. Understand one thing, if you welch out on me, I will make your life a living hell!" he said.

"OK, it's a deal, but please understand that some actions will take a while to fade away.

But I give you my word."

We shook hands and I was brought back to my cell. The next day I tested the deal.

I told one of the guards I wanted to be taken to the law library. He said when everyone else goes, I could go. I told him he better check with the warden, because that ain't the way it's gonna be. He came back in five minutes and took me to the law library. Soon, all the guards knew the score. I go where and when I want to go.

One night at the law library, two Italian guys came to my table. One of them, Pasquale, was a very connected guy. He was connected to one of the Broward County Mafia crime families. He said he can't wait for his lawyer to show up on Monday, as he was out of town, and he did not feel too good, and needed medical attention.

I wrote a petition for an emergency writ for him. He was taken to the courthouse on a Saturday morning and the judge ordered him to be taken to the hospital for treatment. When his lawyer came back, he was released on bond. Pasquale put $100 in my commissary account as a thank you gesture.

One night, Ted Bundy was brought into the law library when I was the only other one there. He wasn't allowed to be there when other inmates were there, but for some reason I was left alone with him. Ted had been representing himself and was doing a shit job. A lot of glaring technical errors. I figured I would give him some advice. He got very nasty with me, and said in a rage:

"I don't need your help, punk! You don't know shit."

"OK, be that way" I said as I bitch-slapped him across the face. "Come anywhere near me, and I will break your neck. I am trying to help you, and this is the way you act?"

He had no balls against men, only with the women he raped and strangled to death. I told him that if he said anything to the guards, he would wish for the death penalty when my people got through with him. If he said anything to the guards, he would be very sorry. Fuck him.

Meanwhile, sixty days had passed on Rolando's motion, and no trial was started, of course. I filed a motion to dismiss. The motion was denied by the trial court. OK, now I filed an appeal with the district court of appeals. I included a copy of the certificate of service signed by the guard that was delivered to the court. The state attorney had claimed they never received it. The appeals court granted my petition and issued a Writ of Prohibition preventing the trial court from proceeding with the case. They had no choice but to dismiss the case based on the violation of the speedy trial rule. Rolando was released, again. This is better than getting laid!

Months are passing quickly. A year has gone by and I am still a pre-trial detainee. We had pursued an insanity defense because I had no other defense. I had admitted the armed robbery during the murder trial, so I can't say I lied. I was seen by several prominent psychologists who said I had a drug-induced psychosis, and that I had criminal tendencies. Duh! The Judge told my attorney that he was not going to buy any insanity defense, and if I am found guilty, he will give me the maximum sentence, 25 years. Yeah, that sounds great.

Pasquale had been picked up on some RICO charges and was back in the jail. I sent word to him that I need to have a "sit down." I wanted to try to find out if there was a contract out on me for the murder case. After all, nobody believes a not guilty verdict. The guards knew who Pasquale was connected with and showed him respect.

He was brought to my cell with his buddy, Vincent. I explained what happened, and why my boss was hit. Pasquale said he owed me and would find out what was on the street. He said you have to watch out for the "Wise Guys," but if he hears of anything, he will have it "squashed".

I thanked him, and he said he would call Mario. He did call Mario a couple of weeks after he got out on bond, and was told there was nothing on the street, and that I shouldn't worry. That was a relief.

More time passed... going on two years. The courts were getting sick of seeing my labels on all the motions I was writing. The state finally offers me a deal. They will drop the armed robbery charge to robbery by force or fear. I will plead guilty to time served and get life probation. My attorney said I would be sent up to Lake Butler for processing, and after about 3 months, I would be released.

He said I could fight the life probation in the future. Meanwhile, this is the best deal I am going to see. I decided to take the deal. This means hanging out in the county jail until the next corrections bus goes up to Lake Butler. I waited and waited and did a lot of thinking about my life. In jail, you can't escape from your thoughts. It can drive you crazy. Memories pop up that you forgot about, sometimes bad memories. You analyze yourself over and over.

"Luzani, get your shit, time to go", yelled Corporal Sanchez.

"Shit, it's 4:30 in the morning," I complained.

Well, I had to get my act together for the bus ride to the joint. This should be a trip to remember.

I rode up with a bunch of lunatics. I met one guy who was on his way to death row to await execution. I was thinking how easily that could have been me. He was placed in a caged-in seat in the front of the bus.

When we arrived at the Lake Butler Reception Center, they brought all of us into a huge room and lined up everyone in a straight line. We all had to bend over and crack a smile, then we had to get nude, get bug sprayed and take a shower, and then they gave us clothes. This whole time we had to always stand on the other side of the Red Line. When we would be outside, in the hot sun, if we stood in the shade, the guards would say, "Get out of my Shade, boy." This is hell. One recurring thought always went through my mind; I don't belong here, I am not like these other guys, I could make something of myself.

My only goal at that point was to stay out of trouble so that I didn't end up with more time. I needed to get out of that place. One thing I learned from jail is that solitude makes you very introspective. You lay around in your bunk all day and watch your life pass by many times over. It can drive you nuts for sure.

My time to finally get out was coming closer. I couldn't wait to get out of there. Then, one day I heard the words I'd been waiting for.

"Luzani, get your stuff together, say your goodbyes, you're going home," said one of the guards.

Wow, this is exciting. I am going to be free man. Free to begin a new life. I was put on a Bus in Gainesville with a few other ex-cons. We all had a brown paper bag with our belongings. The other people on the bus all knew we came from the prison.

It was a very interesting ride to Tampa Airport, where I would catch a flight to Fort Lauderdale. I had made the decision in jail that I never, ever, wanted to go back to jail. I will not contact anybody that I used to know. I will start over from scratch. My mind was made up.

My dad and my sister picked me up at the airport. The plan was that I would work for my dad in sales. I was always great at sales. It's funny that throughout my whole life I was always torn between being in business or being in crime. Even when I was dealing, I would place ads to sell mail order items. I loved the mail-order business. Too bad the crime always won out over doing legitimate business ventures. That's because of the drugs, I am sure of that now.

This is going to be a new beginning for me. I will have a chance to prove myself in the real business world. My dad had been in the surveillance equipment business. He was semi-retired, but had some good accounts, like the Palm Beach Airport.

I started out at $50 a week, living at my dad's house. Soon, I was familiar with all the equipment and could read blueprints. I was making sales calls and getting orders. We also conducted counter surveillance sweeps and checked phone lines for taps. I had a particular talent for making hidden camera items, like a wireless camera in a picture frame.

I went out on counter surveillance sweeps at a pain clinic in West Palm Beach, and in attorney's offices and homes. While doing the pain clinic, I came across a video tape on making silencers. Can you believe this? A doctor thinking about making a silencer, which is only used for one thing: to ice somebody! This doctor was in serious trouble and ended up going to prison. I had special equipment, and I knew my stuff.

My Dad was doing more and more business with the Palm Beach Airport. He was always meeting some guy for lunch. The guy turned out to be the buyer for surveillance equipment.

The business was growing fast. We had to rent a 2,500 square foot warehouse. At the time I had been trying to meet a chick, and after a while, I met a great gal who did not care what kind of car I drove, or that I was obviously not rich. We dated for a while and ended up getting married and having two wonderful kids.

So, there I was, on my way to normalcy, or so I thought. Meanwhile, I had to have my probation modified so that I could travel freely. I wrote my own motion for Modification of Probation and brought it to the court clerk. After all, I practiced law in the big house, remember?

A hearing date was set.

When I went before the judge, he tried to pull some shit.

"Mr. Luzani, what makes you think you are different from all the other convicted felons on Probation? What makes you think you are entitled to have it modified?"

"Your Honor, my attorney told me that it was part of the deal that I made with the court. Are you telling me that my attorney lied?" I said loudly and clearly.

Well, that shut him up, and he signed the Court Order that I prepared, right there on the spot. It felt great. Now I can travel between all the counties without violating the law.

One fateful day my Dad got into a car accident and ended up in the hospital. While in the hospital, he picked up an infection and ended up dying. Before he died, he said to me that I was going to make a lot of money in the business, and that I should use my head. I wasn't sure what he really meant, but it sounded good.

When the buyer from the airport heard that my dad had died, he set up a meeting with me at a local restaurant for lunch. This meeting would start a new chain of events that would control my life for several more years and would take me back to the dark side. He told me that he had an "arrangement," with my dad, and if I wanted to continue to do business with the airport, I would have to continue with the "arrangement."

I wasn't born yesterday, so I knew what he meant. He was getting paid off by my dad, and I knew nothing about it until now. This is against the law, I thought to myself, here we go again. What do I have to do to go straight? Most of our business came out of that airport, so by not playing ball he could put me out of business.

I told him that I am not my father and I don't do business like that.

"Listen, Mr. Clean, it took years to set this up, and you are not going to ruin it," he said.

So, I get up and walk out of the restaurant.

In a couple of days I get a phone call. I am asked to come to a meeting at the airport to discuss our contracts. This would not be an ordinary business meeting. After I checked in with the buyer at his office, I was walked to an old conference room deep down in one of the basement areas. This ain't good I thought to myself. I am brought into a room, where there were four guys sitting at a table. I was told to sit in a chair in front of them.

"Mr. Luzani, we hear that you would like to commit suicide, is that true?" says this big fat Italian looking guy. "We know all about you, so don't play that Goody Two Shoes bullshit, we have come too far to walk away now. You got a problem with making a lot of money, are you insane or something."

The first thought in my mind was that I could just ice these assholes, but I thought I was getting out of a life of crime. Well, here I was again, at a crossroads. Do I go to war, or do I play ball and make a lot of money. Now I had a wife and kids to worry about.

"Listen you guys, don't get all excited. Since you put it so nicely, I can assure you that I will be part of the team. So just relax, but don't try to take advantage of me like you probably did with my dad. We negotiate an all new deal, starting from today, or else count me out," I said as I stood up.

They agreed, and we worked out the numbers. Taxes would have to be paid on any cash I took out of the business. Soon, I was having to raise hundreds of thousands of dollars cash for the payoffs. I had to open more than 10 checking accounts. It was becoming an all-consuming thing. I could not raise enough cash, so I had to have other people help me. I write a check to them, and they give me the cash. Now, I have two other people that know about this "arrangement." After a while, and several contracts, these two employees of mine started to extort money from me. That's right, now I am the victim of a crime. Keep in mind that these two guys did not know of my background. They had no idea with whom they were dealing.

After I gave one guy more than $150,000 in cash, I tried to cut back on their extortion attempts. One guy, the old guy, was reasonable. He wanted to retire, and he would back off with a final payment of $75,000. The other guy was going to play hard ball. He demanded to have a meeting with the airport guy to hit him up for money. I spoke with the airport guy, and he agreed to the meeting to be held at my office.

When we all took a seat at my conference table. My employee, Johnnie, says to the guy,

"I want you to give me money, or I will turn all of you in".

The guy says, "Fuck you," and gets up to leave the room.

Johnnie gets in front of him and won't let him leave the room. He pulls out a .38 caliber, and orders us to sit down.

He tells the airport guy that he has a video tape of him taking bribes.

Now, I know right away that he has no such tape, but he does have the gun, and I don't.

Time to take control.

"Hey Johnnie, is this any way to treat our guest? I am sure that after I have a talk with the airport people, that we can include you in at a higher level," I said.

I looked over to the airport guy, and he understood what I was trying to do, and he agreed that we can work this out without going crazy.

Johnnie says, "I will give you a little time to come up with a plan."

The next day, I am called in to a meeting at the airport. I am brought into a parking garage and escorted to a limousine. There were a bunch of pissed off guys in there. These are the guys that nobody sees. They run everything that has to do with the big bucks. They are on the airport payroll, and have the security badges, but they are all part of organized crime. Now, they are pissed at me.

"Sal, we heard about the incident the other day at your office. This is your guy, and you have to take care of this problem," says Mr. Kane.

Roberto says, "Sal if this guy goes too far, we could all take a fall. This means that if we take a fall because of your guy, you will pay the price, Capeche?"

I say, "Are you telling me that you want me to dust this guy?"

I thought I was retired from that life. Why can't I get away from this criminal stuff. Damn it, what am I going to do? Now I have a wife and kids. I just can't do anything I want to now. But this is clearly a deep threat, on many levels.

I think I am going to have to take this guy out. God forgive me, but this guy represents a threat, and has to be neutralized. I will have to make this a mission. I will do this all on my own. Nobody will know anything. Johnnie will just not be around anymore. I gathered up the materials I would need to make a silencer and picked up a couple of good pieces. I stayed at the warehouse late at night and did my thing, and produced, once again, silenced weapons. This time they were a little more upgraded than the last time.

All I had to do was set up a meeting with Johnnie supposedly to give him cash. I arranged for a meeting at a rest area off I-75, near the Everglades. We had met there before, so he was not hesitant. Nighttime would be the best time, but we could meet as it is getting dark, then I will dust him. I brought iced tea with me for us to drink. Iced Tea is a diuretic and he will have to take a leak in the restroom.

The place was empty and nobody was around. We bullshitted for a while and drank the tea. After a while, he had to take a leak. I followed him in and popped him in the noggin. I dragged him out and dumped him in the canal, where I could see many alligator eyes shining in the moonlight, as they pierced through the surface of the water in the canal, watching my every move.

This was a quiet, and fast hit. I was out of there very quickly and no evidence was left behind. I had a rented car with fake plates. The next day, I was contacted by Mr. Big from the airport mob. They met me at a restaurant in Lake Worth, which was mob-owned. Vincent brings me back into a party room where all the bosses are eating Italian stuff.

"Sit down Sal, join us for some great lunch."

Well, I knew I better not insult anybody, so I said thanks, and took a seat.

"Sal, you did good. We want you to know that you can come to us if you ever need a favor. All we ask is that you keep a tight rein on your guys."

"I will make sure we don't go through this again," I said.

Now how the hell did they find out about this so soon before it hit the news. Freaky.

On the way home, I kept thinking that I have to find a way to get out of this business. This negative life will have no end if I can't extricate myself.

Back at work, people wondered what happened to Johnnie. His body was never found. He just faded away, as did the problems he created.

I set up a hidden camera in a book on a shelf in my office. I videotaped the buyer putting stacks of cash in his suit pockets. This was to be my insurance policy.

How ironic is this? I inherited criminal activity from my dad. I never knew he had criminal tendencies, I guess it runs in the family. This is nuts.

Now the business is getting really big from the multi-million dollar contracts we are getting. We had to move into a 32,000 square foot warehouse with 28 employees. I am enjoying the money, but I am not happy. I worry all of the time. I know that this could all end tomorrow. The business was built on graft and corruption, and I had no choice.

I gave these assholes millions in cash, and paid hundreds of thousands of dollars to the IRS. I figured that I would try to sell the business while I had some good contracts, without the airport guys knowing what I was up to. Many potential buyers came to look at this business. I cooked the books so that it would look fantastic. I had several bites, but when they ran my background, they would all back off. Being a convicted felon is no good.

Eventually, I found a group who wanted to buy the business, or should I say they found me? They just wanted to buy it for a tax write off. In eight months, they were out of business.

They left town owing me over $900,000. They also left me on as the personal guarantor on a $400,000 credit line. Who do you think the bank came after? That's right, good old Salvatore gets screwed again. I was forced into bankruptcy. I lost everything I owned, and I mean everything. Turned out to be a good time for a divorce, as my wife and I were drifting apart. So, there I was: broke, no savings, nothing.

I needed a job. I tried to get a job in my trade and had some great interviews. When they ran my background, they wouldn't even return my calls. This is getting scary. I thought about how I was going to survive. I was at a very low point in my life once again. I learned how to cry and how to pray on my knees, asking for strength to get through the next day. Sometimes, I would pray not to wake up the next day.

I kicked around in jobs that would hire convicted felons, commission-only jobs like car or telephone sales. I would last through the training pay period, then disappear. I was miserable.

Then one day I read a book called "The Secret" about the laws of attraction and the power of positive thinking. It changed my life. I trained myself to think the opposite of the way I used to be. I became optimistic and not a pessimist.

I made labels up and a flier for the surveillance equipment business. I would hit the streets at night and saturate office and industrial parks with my sales literature. Soon, I was getting calls, booking work. Then the economy took a crap.

I have been surviving through the worst economy since the Depression, but that's okay. I made a deal with myself and I'm sticking to it. No more crime for me, no way!

But don't count me out. Remember, I am like the Phoenix, rising from the ashes! One thing will always remain the same with me; I don't give up and I don't quit. Maybe I'll become an author someday and write a book about my life.

Weeks went by and I managed to eke out a living. I can't live like this. I have an idea, and it is not legit by any means. You know how people talk about making money, well I had that thought, I will literally MAKE MONEY. That is something I had always wanted to do. Print my own money.

Printing technology has come a long way. I contacted some of the guys from my old crew. These guys are always ready to take a chance to make some big bucks, especially since we can print our own bucks.

We would all chip in some bucks and take a printing course at a local vocational school. We would say that we are going to open a print shop. It could take up to a year to learn enough to start printing some money. We would purchase used, but in good condition, printing machines, camera equipment to make great printing plates and set up shop in a small warehouse.

We all thought that this is very doable, even if it is a Federal crime. I had connections in the mob that would take all we can print, but it has to be really good.

Months passed and we were all learning as much as we could absorb about printing. It was getting close to the end of the course so we needed to start looking for a base of operations. We also needed to get commercial printing customers and advertise so we looked legit.

If we play our cards right, we can make enough money to retire and buy some business for fun. So, here we are: me, Vinny, Roberto, Jake, and Bernard. Five guys that can handle anything, or so I thought. We had a website being built for the new printing business. This would be a fun project.

Sorry to disappoint you if you were hoping I could go straight. I finally have a chance to make some real bucks, hehe. But don't despair, I will turn this into a great opportunity to straighten out my act.

The problem is that when you are working with other people, things happen that you did not plan on. Like one of the crew's girlfriend said something to one of the guys about making money the easy way.

This is a clear security breach and could jeopardize the whole thing. Sure, I could just dust the chick and the guy also, but I don't want to do that stuff anymore. We could also abandon these premises, but we could still be tracked because of this chick.

So I decided to call a meeting with everybody and tell them that we are all going to have to take a Polygraph exam (sound familiar?) to keep on keeping on. Otherwise we cannot proceed, it is too risky. I know a retired Miami detective who does Polygraph exams.

If anybody refuses to take the Polygraph, it will fuck up everything. Especially since information could be elicited that was unexpected and maybe one of my guys went rogue. I think I will have to be strapped for this sit-down.

I set the exams up in a friend's cabin near the everglades fishing camp. There was no telling how this will end. The meeting was set for 8pm. Everybody arrived on time but Roberto and his chick. An hour goes by and nothing. We all look at each other like this is very bad. Everybody came strapped in case something happened. I had a vest in my car, so I went out and put it on.

I was notified by a sentry of mine that a car was on its way to me with a car full of 4-5 guys. These roads are pitch black at night and never traveled, except for criminals mostly. We now have minutes to get ready for an impending attack.

The guys know what is up and we all know what we must do. We bail out of the cabin to get in positions outside.

We see vehicle lights fast approaching and we all switch to night vision goggles. As the attack vehicle, an SUV, comes barreling into the property, we open fire killing all the occupants. This was not time to stop and ask questions.

Everybody has been through this before. We each know our job. Get the stiffs into some of these canals where the gators will eat them. Take the vehicle and drive it into a canal deep in the Glades.

Roberto and his chick were in the SUV dead. So that takes care of them. He was a bad apple. Now we will have to bail out of the warehouse we rented and maybe relocate to the Orlando area.

This will be a setback, but not insurmountable. So this crazy story does not end here. Keep in touch and I will let you know what the Salvatore Luzani Crew is up to. Maybe we will leave the country, who knows. I will try to fight my Criminal Tendencies….. yeah right!

Sign-up for the newsletter on my website:
www.criminaltendenciesbook.com

CPSIA information can be obtained
at www.ICGtesting.com
Printed in the USA
BVHW082131060123
655722BV00002B/273